DIABLO®

BOOK OF ADRIA

A DIABLO BESTIARY

Written by Robert Brooks & Matt Burns

Contents

The Frozen Sea

Xiansai

Scosglen

Túr Dúlra

Dry Steppes

Kehjistan

Caldeum

Kul

Ureh

Kurast

Swamp Lands

Viz-jun

Sea of Light

ary

Man's pleasures give way to pain.

✠

His truths are buried in the shroud of lies.

✠

It is this time when Hell shall reign.

✠

While all of man dies.

Seven Evils spawned of seven heads.

✠

Seven realms birthed from death,

✠

Infested, unending, cycles upon cycles.

Introduction

What is power?

Think on it for a moment. Picture it in your mind's eye.

What do you see? A blade? A spell? A vault of gold? The emperor of Kehjistan on his gilded throne? A Zakarum high priest with his fine raiment and bejeweled scepter?

I see a twig of Entsteig pine. Yes, just a little twig of that coarse bark with dry, green needles. As common in the forests as salt in the sea. A poison made from its sap can kill a man in three days but rub the bark on a wound and it can purify infections. Grind the needles into a powder and they are the primary reagent in a blindness curse.

That is power. Not a blade. Not a crown. Not a fortune. Not even that pine twig. Power is knowing how to use those things to get what you want.

The world around us is a vault of riches waiting to be plundered. Every creature, every plant, and every culture can serve us, willingly or not, in our goal to aid the Lords of the Burning Hells. But the Coven cannot use these weapons if we do not study them.

That is why I have collected all that I have learned from my travels and the knowledge of those who came before us into this codex. Read it. Learn about our allies and our enemies. Learn of the dangers that await us, and how we might turn them to our advantage. Know this world well, and you will always have something useful to offer the demons.

The final war between the High Heavens and the Burning Hells is coming, and if our masters do not prevail, we will suffer a fate worse than death.

I have seen the Coven's uncertain destiny in the fire. Through the flames, the demon lords whisper to me of what is to come. They have told me of two outcomes. In one, the Lords of Hell recognize our worth and we rule alongside them. In another, they see us as less than useless and torment our souls for eternity.

What path we find ourselves on when the storm comes is up to us.

It took far too long before I understood that Diablo was the voice whispering to me in the flames.

The Lord of Terror had been watching me, testing me. I had felt his power. Primal and ancient. Far beyond anything the Coven had discovered. I thought the wisdom I had learned from the flames was for all those who sought it.

But when the fire called me to the town of Tristram, I knew the truth. Diablo had chosen me. Only me.

I left the Coven and never looked back.

The people of Tristram did not know that Diablo had been imprisoned beneath their feet. Not until it was too late. His darkness suffocated the little town. It drove King Leoric and his servants to bloody madness. I saw all of it as a promise of what I could have—what I could do—if I pledged myself to Diablo.

I was unsure of how to serve the Lord of Terror until Prince Aidan arrived.

He had returned from war to find his home darkened, his father turned to the undead, and his little brother possessed by Diablo. He showed tenacity and courage. He faced the terrors of Tristram alone, and he triumphed. Then, having achieved so much, he suffered a very human moment of arrogance: he believed that he could contain Diablo within his soul.

For a time, it seemed that he would succeed. I sat with Aidan and lay with him at night, nurturing him as I knew I must. It took time before I saw the change. His eyes would flicker, his lips would twist upward, and his voice would deepen. Then I would speak with the Lord of Terror himself.

Diablo told me his plans. He set me to act in case of his failure.

And so, I did. As Diablo continued to possess Aidan, he became known as **THE DARK WANDERER.** We remained together until he departed Tristram. I think he loved me, in his way. Perhaps I even loved him, knowing what he would bestow upon me.

A vessel. Something powerful enough to contain the souls of not just Diablo, but all his brothers and sisters.

And now that Aidan has been slain, this vessel growing within me is the true hope for the End of Days.

She is the key to Diablo's return.

I do not know how I will bring him back yet, but one thing is certain: This book must never be returned to the Coven. They are not worthy of its secrets.

-1-
The Coven and its Rites

The Coven is not the first order to work with demons. Others have had that honor. But there is an advantage to not being the first: We can learn from the mistakes of those who came before us. We can refine the methods of ancient demonologists and revive their forbidden spellwork.

We should also look beyond demonology. I have studied witchcraft, as have many of you. Those arts will be useful to our cause, as will the spells of the mage clans, the illusions of the Ammuit, the elemental fury of the Zann Esu, the enchantments of the Ennead, and the divination rituals of the Taan. Even the magic of the Zakarum has some value.

It does not matter that these groups are not aligned with the Burning Hells. It does not matter that we disagree with their beliefs. The only question we should ask ourselves is this: are they powerful?

The followers of Zakarum are mindless zealots, but their inquisitors are effective at interrogation and torture. We would be fools to ignore such methods simply because of their origin.

Remember, too, that we are free from the rules that bind these religions and cultures. Where they are limited by tradition, we are not.

The only way we will prevail in the coming war between the High Heavens and the Burning Hells is if we embrace all this world has to offer. We must mold what we take into a new system of power. The old leaders of the Coven started this process, but they did not go far enough.

If they had, they would still be alive.

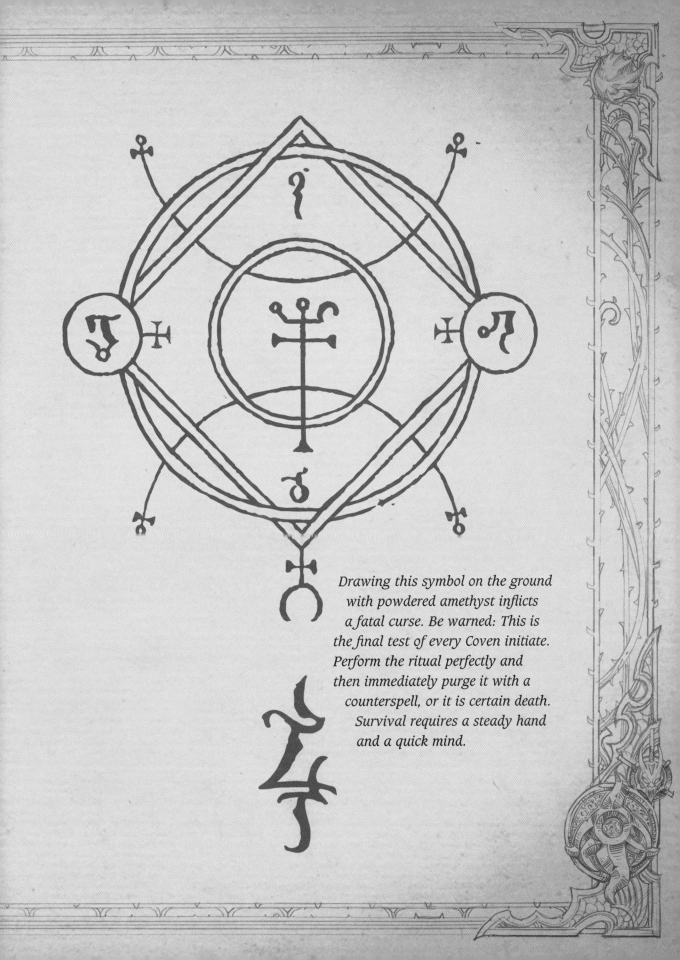

Drawing this symbol on the ground
with powdered amethyst inflicts
a fatal curse. Be warned: This is
the final test of every Coven initiate.
Perform the ritual perfectly and
then immediately purge it with a
counterspell, or it is certain death.
Survival requires a steady hand
and a quick mind.

Origins

We were once the Cult of the Triune, servants of the three Prime Evils: **Diablo**, **Mephisto**, and **Baal**. Now we are the Coven, a gathering of lost souls seeking our destiny in the fires of the Eternal Conflict.

It feels strange to write about ourselves like this, but it is important to <u>know where we fit in the final destiny of Sanctuary</u>. Or where we do not. Lords and peasants alike refer to "cultists" with contempt. They think we have devoted ourselves to a false cause, and that our willingness to die speaks of a diseased mind. Their disdain shall be repaid ten times over—not by us, but by the future we will create.

Or where we do not.

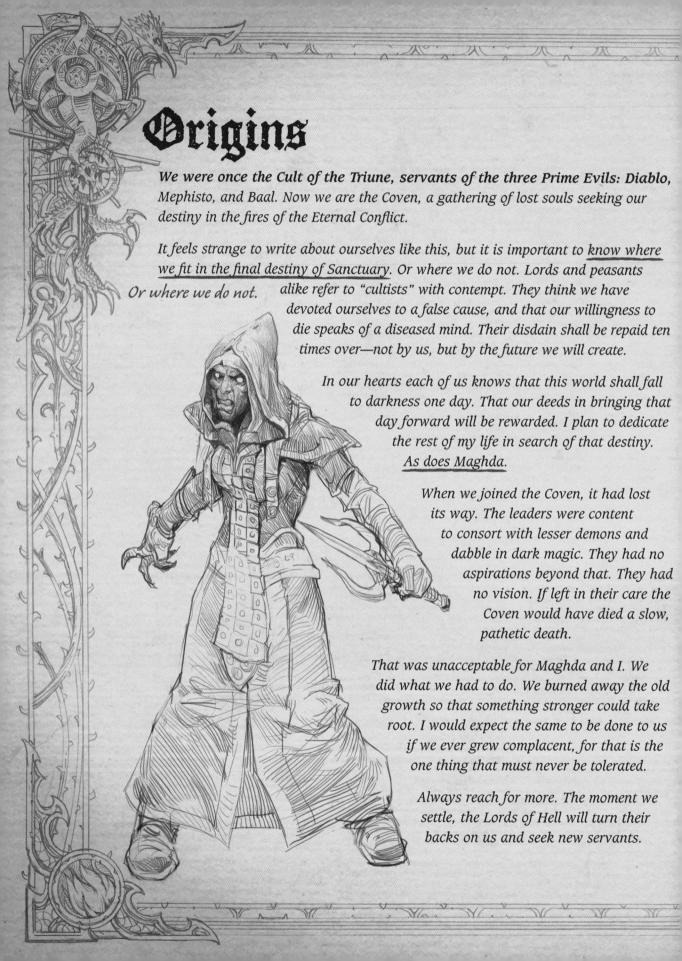

In our hearts each of us knows that this world shall fall to darkness one day. That our deeds in bringing that day forward will be rewarded. I plan to dedicate the rest of my life in search of that destiny. <u>As does Maghda.</u>

When we joined the Coven, it had lost its way. The leaders were content to consort with lesser demons and dabble in dark magic. They had no aspirations beyond that. They had no vision. If left in their care the Coven would have died a slow, pathetic death.

That was unacceptable for Maghda and I. We did what we had to do. We burned away the old growth so that something stronger could take root. I would expect the same to be done to us if we ever grew complacent, for that is the one thing that must never be tolerated.

Always reach for more. The moment we settle, the Lords of Hell will turn their backs on us and seek new servants.

I was always more powerful than Maghda but that did not mean I was greater. Neither of us were. We complemented each other. I, the fire and the passion. She, the insight and the control.

But she grew too comfortable. Too complacent. She believed we were nearing the mountain peak, but we were still stumbling through the foothills.

When I left her to answer Diablo's call, I did not feel sadness. I felt a burden being lifted from my shoulders.

Days and Months

We must always begin our work during the correct days and months. Time is a cycle that passes through different phases, each with a unique effect on magic and the creatures that inhabit this world as well as the Burning Hells.

Kathon—The 15th day of Kathon is the crimson moon. The Triune refers to this phenomenon as the Eye of Baal. During this time of the month destructive spells are more potent but harder to control. Sacrifices are best performed under the crimson moon.

Solmoneth and Montaht—The months when day and night are equal. It is a time of dreams and visions. Scrying spells and illusions are more powerful in Solmoneth and Montaht than at any other time of the year. This is also when Belial and his minions seem most active.

Ostara—The month of rebirth, when healing spells and elixirs are most potent.

Vasan and Lycanum—In Kehjistan these are the months of sowing and fertility. They represent the duality between male and female. I also believe they represent the conflict between angels and demons. Do not parlay with the creatures of the Burning Hells during this time for they will be erratic and easy to anger.

Kale Monath—The month of plagues and pestilence. I have found brewing poisons during this time to be most effective. Reagents also bind more easily.

Lunasadh—The "baker's month" when crops are harvested, and food is plenty. Demons aligned with Azmodan seem easier to contact in the latter half of the month.

Jerharan and Damhar—These months are where the barrier between our world and other realms weakens, specifically the days at the end of Jerharan and the beginning of Damhar. It is the ideal time to summon demons from the Burning Hells.

Ratham—The ideal time to summon, bind, or commune with spirits as it is the month of the dead. These acts are best conducted during the new moon.

Esunar—The month of fire, water, air, earth and other elemental powers. There is a connection between magic and the physical world in this month making it the best time to create amulets or perform other enchantments on objects.

Invocations and Summoning Rituals

Words have power. Some more than others. Every spell or rite we perform is a combination of these elements: reagents, intent, and focus. But what we say is perhaps the most important part. The correct order and pronunciation of incantations must be as familiar to us as our own names.

When dealing with the minions of the Hells, names are crucial. Speaking a demon's name will allow us to contact it, as well as give us some amount of power over the creature.

There are three names we must learn before any others. The first is <u>Al'Diabolos</u>, the true name of Diablo, Lord of Terror. The next is <u>Tor'Baalos</u>, the true name of Baal, Lord of Destruction. The last is <u>Dul'Mephistos</u>, the true name of Mephisto, Lord of Hatred. Other cultures refer to them by different names. The Umbaru people speak of a destructive spirit named Khoyassa. They do not know it is actually Baal, but the name they have given him still holds power.

When communing with a demon that serves Diablo, speak the Lord of Terror's true name. The same applies to the other Prime Evils and their respective minions. Pronounce the name of the correct demon lord loudly and clearly. If we do not, the creature we are contacting may see it as a slight against their master and lash out.

Sacrificial blood must come from young and vigorous humans or beasts whose life energies are potent. Never use sick or dying creatures, for they will weaken our rituals and likely anger the demons we are trying to contact.

The first demons that most of us learn to summon are simple-minded, but powerful. Invoking the true names of greater demons is an effective way of exerting our willpower over them. But that will not change their nature. They are like wild beasts. It is best to set them loose and stand out of their way.

For summoning, always use three, four, or seven people. These are numbers of power that represent the hierarchy of the Hells: three is the number of the Prime Evils, four the Lesser Evils, and seven the combination of the two. Never attempt to summon a demon alone.

Some of the Coven believe that if we invite a minion of the Hells inside ourselves, we ascend to a higher plane of existence. I suspect that we become nothing, and are merely replaced by a demon.

They were always too eager to trade their lives— their sense of self— for table scraps of demonic power. A one-sided exchange. That is not my path.

I gave him my blood and soul. In return, Diablo offered me the power to achieve the destiny I had always known was mine.

The answers lie with the ancient mage, Zoltun Kulle.

Various historical accounts cast him as a monster, a visionary, or a misguided genius. I believe he was all these things.

Kulle was recruited into the Horadrim, the order of mages created by Archangel Tyrael to hunt the Prime Evils. But serving as Tyrael's pawn was not to be Kulle's fate. His battles with demons darkened him, and he set off on a quest to make himself a god.

He had discovered the secret of humanity, that we were created by a union between angels and demons. The first generations of these children were called the nephalem, and they were extraordinarily powerful. Each generation grew weaker as time went on, but the power did not disappear completely. It still lurked in the blood of every man, woman, and child.

Kulle found a way to unlock that power, but the Horadrim hunted him down before he could finish his work. Whether he is truly dead or banished to a different realm is another question.

But his fate does not matter, only what he learned. And what he created.

THE BLACK SOULSTONE. It is the answer I have been seeking.

Kulle wanted to use it to mark the souls of angels and demons alike, trapping their essences in the crystal and using that power to awaken his own latent nephalem blood. However, he was unable to activate it in his lifetime.

He was a fool to aim so short. It has the capacity for so much more.

I have been dreaming of the soulstone. Every night.

Not as it is, but as it will be.

Trembling with the spirits of the Prime and Lesser Evils who scream from their prison. They shake with rage when they realize what Diablo is planning. But it is too late. Far too late.

Before they can act, the spirits are channeled into the vessel. My master consumes them all. Becomes them all. Mortal flesh burns away to reveal his greatest form.

The Prime Evil.

I can make this dream a reality. With Kulle's spells to mark the souls of the Evils, and the Black Soulstone to contain them, I can bring this vision to life.

– 11 –
The Dead and the Damned

Life does not endure. Our flesh fails, our skin wrinkles, our limbs ache, our lungs struggle to draw breath, our minds wither, then our hearts churn slow, then not at all.

~~All things~~ on this world shall die. *Most things*

Yet, death need not be the end. Our lords and masters have told us so, and the power they have taught us is our proof. Any dead creature has gifts to offer the Coven. There is power in blood, in decaying flesh and bone, in ribs bleaching in the Kehjistani sun, in skulls drifting along the bottom of the Twin Seas. The discarded forms of mortal creatures can be used or reused in countless ways. It is an art ripe for experimentation.

But the remains of the dead contain only a fraction of the usefulness their spirits once had. The power of <u>souls</u> is extraordinary. They are vibrating knots of energy that rejuvenate themselves, burning brightly and for far longer than any temple of flesh could. Even when siphoning tremendous draughts of power from them, if a spark of existence remains, it will shine on.

Souls instinctively yearn for a vessel to call their own, whether it be a mortal creature or a temporary construct. Most will even accept imprisonment inside a body they do not control, for it is better to know the sensation of flesh than not. Sometimes the soul is strong enough to wrest control from its host. This is the crux of possession.

Possessed humans are excellent subjects for experiments as you can draw out multiple souls for any use you desire. Give the unsuspecting victim a tea made of oakleaf bark laced with powdered human bone marrow to determine whether they truly harbor multiple souls. It is lightly poisonous, and the sickness will make it difficult for the host to maintain their defenses against the intruding souls, thus making detection easy.

There is abundant power in the bodies and spirits of the dead. But beware the teachings of those who claim to serve the "balance" between life and death. Those fools are known as necromancers, and they have little to offer us. We do not seek balance. We seek domination. We seek victory.

Risen Dead

The dead may rise from their graves for many reasons. The presence of a powerful demon, a convocation, or a source of corruption can all stir them. Some of these dead wander the world in silence until the magic that reanimates them fades away. Others take up weapons and hunt down anything that still lives.

A risen dead strong enough to walk the earth is a creature that can be drained of its power. Doing so in the month of Ratham—especially on the seventh day—produces the best results.

Power from a risen dead can be stored in daggers, amulets, rings, or almost any other object. Purify the item of any residual energies by washing it in a copper pot filled with water, a pinch of Death's Breath, and the blood of a young pack beast.

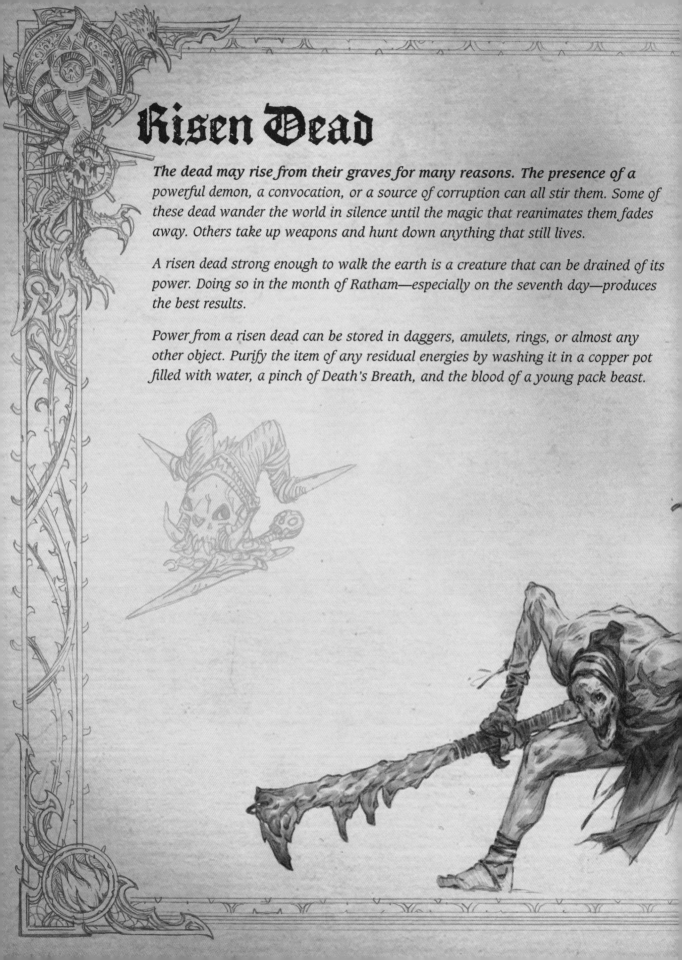

Dune Dervish

The state of these poor beings should serve as a warning to us all. They were once Vizjerei mages who conducted arcane rituals in the deserts of Kehjistan hoping to summon a lieutenant of the Burning Hells. Their "success" not only ended their lives but cursed their eternal souls. They wander the deserts, hunting on instinct alone. There is little to learn from them but caution.

Avoid contact with the dervishes while traveling the deserts. <u>Wear a cloak of deerskin branded with Ammuit runes</u> to become invisible to the creatures.

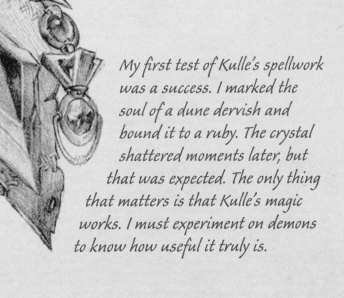

My first test of Kulle's spellwork was a success. I marked the soul of a dune dervish and bound it to a ruby. The crystal shattered moments later, but that was expected. The only thing that matters is that Kulle's magic works. I must experiment on demons to know how useful it truly is.

Enslaved Nightmare

These creatures were once human. Like many others, they sought to wield the power of the Burning Hells for their own purposes. But such things always come at a price. The wills of these selfish fools were no match for the Lords of Hell. Their minds were broken, their bodies brutalized, and their souls leashed to their master forever. At least they are capable of following orders or killing on command, else they would have been discarded.

Over and over, I see that it is better to set the price before accepting a gift from the Lords of Hell. We should proceed carefully on our journeys.

Ghosts

None should ever doubt the raw potential of a soul. Especially not after seeing one of these wraiths. Strong or weak, when humans die before they are ready, their souls will try to cling to this realm. Devoid of conscious thought their continued existence is a scream of denial. They care for nothing but their own lingering rage.

Some angry spirits will cling to any corpse that still has its muscles and sinew intact, puppeting them in a repulsive imitation of life. <u>They are instruments of terror and little more.</u> Better to use these creatures for a purpose than to let them wander aimlessly.

But that has proven very useful indeed . . .

The steps to commune with a spirit are such: first, mark a circle of binding around its resting place; second, take an onyx dagger and coat it three times with Kehjistani sage oil; last, embed the dagger half into the ground at the southern edge of the circle and cast a spell to summon the spirit to your side.

Gargantua

Some cultures devote themselves to raising the dead.
The necromancers are one such group. Another is the
Umbaru people of the Teganze Jungle. Their witch doctors
perform rites that animate corpses to command in battle.
But these risen soldiers are not always undead hounds and
shambling corpses. The witch doctors have the unique ability to
create servants called gargantua—corpses infused with so much
Umbaru magic that they transform into powerful giants.

The witch doctors claim that by respecting and honoring the
dead they are capable of feats like creating gargantua. I
think this is a story they tell themselves to hide from the
truth. The dead are mindless creatures. They have no
need for honor or respect. They serve whoever has the
power to control them, be it a witch doctor or a demon.

The Umbaru use magically imbued mojos to enhance
their power and strengthen their hold over the risen dead.
Some of these mojos are dolls. Others are body parts or
artifacts. Witch doctors place special importance on items
that were in someone's possession at death. They believe
that these items become a bridge between the world of the
living and the Unformed Lands.

Skeletal Guardian

The skeletal guardians are far more powerful than most risen dead.
These creatures, once nothing more than a pile of bones, were granted life by enterprising mages and gifted with the ability to wield powerful magic. Creating one takes considerable time as well as rare and expensive reagents.

During the golden age of the mage clans, the skeletal guardians were created to protect the estates and vaults of wealthy individuals. Wherever one of these risen dead lingers there is likely something valuable nearby.

It is not wise to confront a guardian directly. Weaken the magic that animates them first. Approach the creature at sunrise and chant the Elegy of the Damned in its presence. This will confuse the guardian long enough to safely pass by it.

Though the Coven could learn how to make skeletal guardians, I do not believe we should. A dozen shambling corpses can unleash as much destruction as a single guardian, and with much less effort.

Mage clans take great pride in creating these guardians, often outfitting them in ornaments and armor. Useless gestures. The vanity of mages never ceases to amaze me.

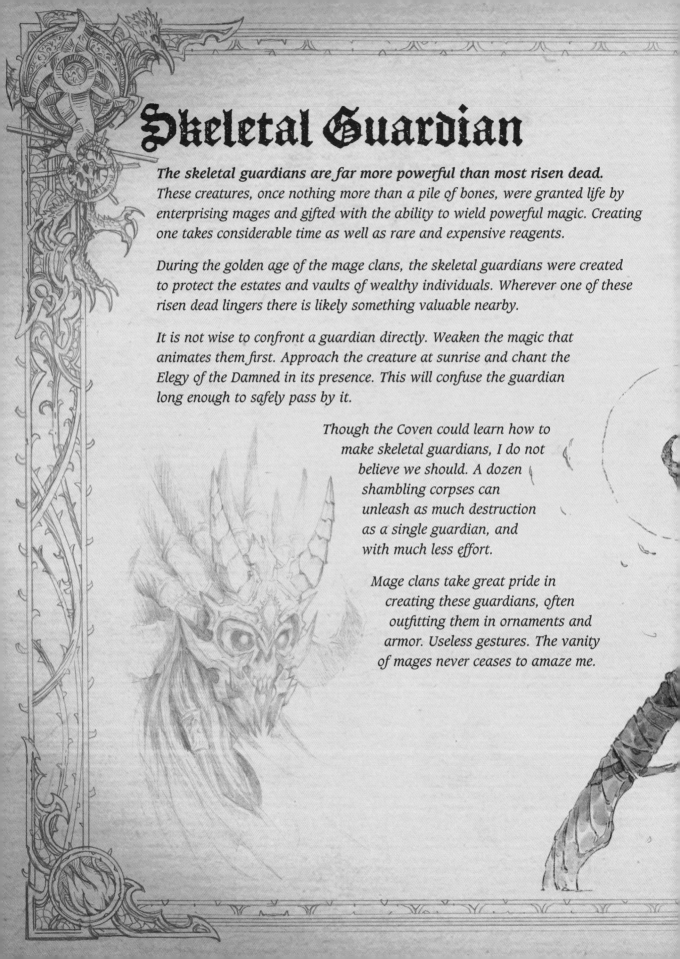

The memories of my time in Tristram are sharper than any others I have.

If I close my eyes, I can see my hut at the edge of town. I barely knew the people I met, but I remember exactly how they looked. The things they said. The potions and salves they bought from me.

My memories of the dead rising in Tristram are even clearer. When I saw them shambling through the forests, I realized they were the product of true power.

It was not the number of the risen dead, though there were many. Any necromancer or witch doctor can bring a corpse to life. It was the air in the village. The way it felt. The sense of dread that hung over everything. It darkened the hearts of all who lived there. Even King Leoric, who so many thought was wise and just. He was a devout follower of the Zakarum faith; a man who always sought peace and stability.

Perhaps it was his desire for those things that made him weak. A king who expects loyalty fears betrayal. A father who loves his family fears losing them. A believer who finds comfort in his faith fears that he will discover it has all been a lie.

Diablo sensed these hidden fears in Leoric. He used them to break the king's mind and turn him into a bloody tyrant.

When Leoric's loyal knights abandoned their oaths and cut him down, it did not stop the chaos. It fed the disorder. Every act of violence and hate fueled it.

Everything Leoric had feared became real. When he was reborn as the SKELETON KING, he transformed into the embodiment of terror.

No one could save Tristram. The people there never understood that. Not Cain. Not Prince Aidan. Not the others who remained in town to stop the chaos.

Tristram was already lost. It was gone the moment my master's influence slipped into the minds of Leoric and his people. The moment he sensed the king's fears and made them into living nightmares. Diablo defeated the people of Tristram before they even knew of his presence.

How could anyone ever stand against a force like that?

With his dying breath, Leoric cursed the **KNIGHTS** who had turned on him. He damned them to spend eternity like him—as skeletal horrors. Even though Leoric spoke the curse, it was not his power. It was a gift from my master.

I still remember seeing my first **WRETCHED MOTHER**. She had been one of Queen Asylla's handmaidens. A young girl. Pretty. We had met once. She called me a witch. She said what I did was unnatural, that I had no virtue in my soul.

Diablo's power twisted her into a ravenous fiend. I saw her eating a fallen soldier. Pulling flesh away from bone in long strips. Our eyes met, and for a moment she recognized me. There was fear in her eyes. And hate. Perhaps it was only my imagination. I watched while she vomited up her meal and the pieces congealed together to form a new undead creature.

I left the pretty girl to her virtuous work.

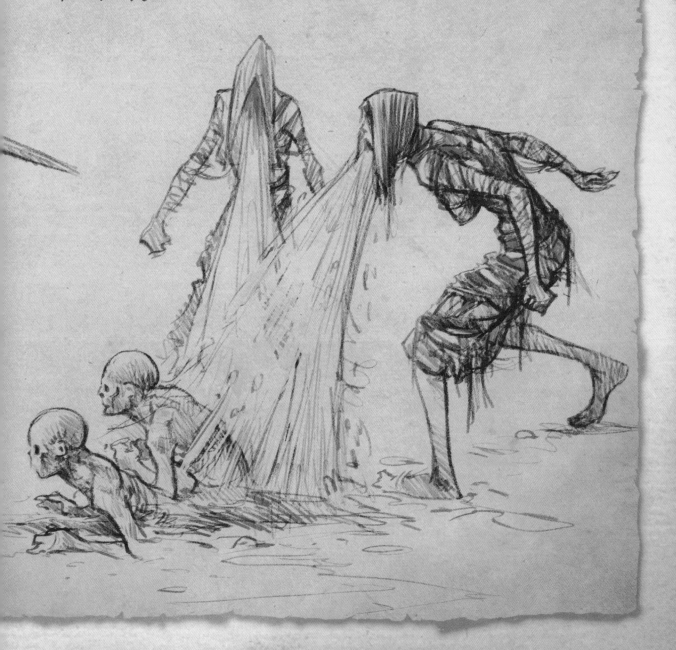

– III –

The Creatures of Sanctuary and Realms Beyond

How many beasts walk this world?

Some scholars have wasted their lives searching for the answer.

The creatures of the world are simply too great in number. That is good for us. It means the tools we have at our disposal are limitless. It is not our purpose to document every beast, but to study and use the ones that have something we need.

We can even learn much from simply observing them. Every creature, no matter how insignificant, exists because it has a strength. Most are quick, clever, dangerous, or a combination of these things. If they were not, they would never survive the harsh and unforgiving wilds.

We must understand the inner workings of these creatures. Nature and magic are an interwoven tapestry. The tides, the seasons, and the movements of the stars are all connected to the beings of this world. They are bound to the flesh and bone of all beasts. They influence each other, just as they influence humans.

Sightings of certain beasts have meaning, both good and ill. The time when creatures migrate, hunt, or mate can be a sign of when is best to perform certain rites.

Even beyond their symbolic value, these creatures have practical uses. Some can be used as bait for larger predators. Some can be harvested for reagents required in spells and rituals. Others can be enslaved as guardians.

All have a role to play in the days to come.

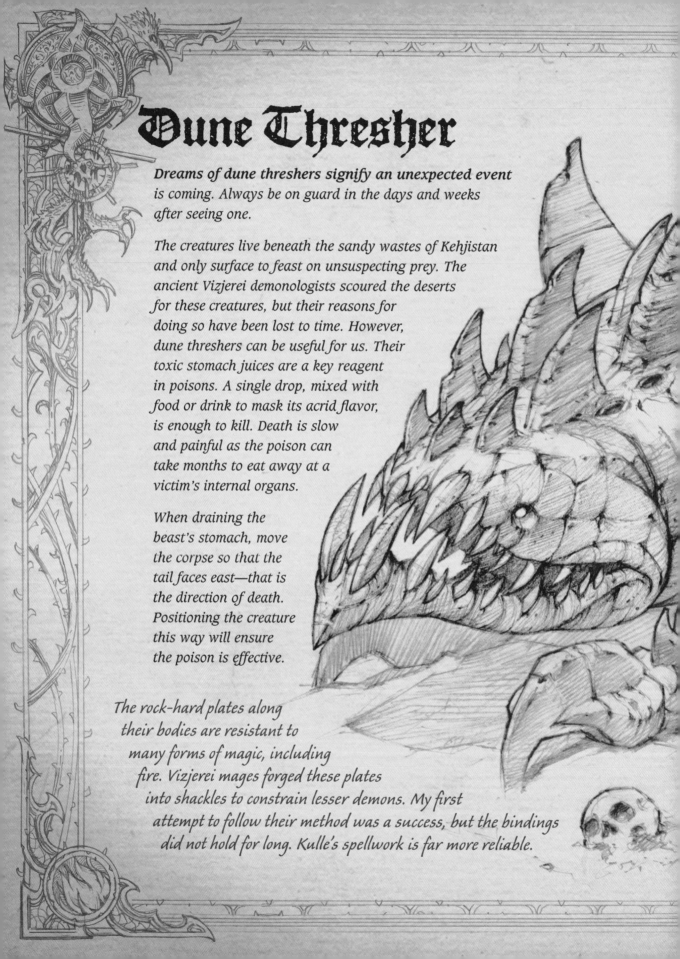

Dune Thresher

Dreams of dune threshers signify an unexpected event is coming. Always be on guard in the days and weeks after seeing one.

The creatures live beneath the sandy wastes of Kehjistan and only surface to feast on unsuspecting prey. The ancient Vizjerei demonologists scoured the deserts for these creatures, but their reasons for doing so have been lost to time. However, dune threshers can be useful for us. Their toxic stomach juices are a key reagent in poisons. A single drop, mixed with food or drink to mask its acrid flavor, is enough to kill. Death is slow and painful as the poison can take months to eat away at a victim's internal organs.

When draining the beast's stomach, move the corpse so that the tail faces east—that is the direction of death. Positioning the creature this way will ensure the poison is effective.

The rock-hard plates along their bodies are resistant to many forms of magic, including fire. Vizjerei mages forged these plates into shackles to constrain lesser demons. My first attempt to follow their method was a success, but the bindings did not hold for long. Kulle's spellwork is far more reliable.

Approach slain dune threshers with care.
Their jagged tails can continue thrashing
for some time after death.

Golem

Turning bits of flesh, dirt, metal, and other inanimate materials into golems is an art the necromancers have perfected over their long history. I first saw it happen in the forests near Westmarch. I had been following a necromancer for a chance to steal the spell books she carried. One night, a pack of scavengers descended on her camp. The necromancer knelt and drew a blade across her flesh, all while chanting the Prayer of Rathma. There was great ritual to the process. The blood that poured from her wound slowly changed. It became a writhing mass of flesh and sinew. A thing without form. Then it grew legs, arms, and a head. A giant bound to its creator's will. The golem tore through the scavengers with the strength of ten men, but controlling it required intense concentration.

The necromancer was so focused on commanding her golem, I could have taken her spell books right then. But I wanted to see more. I wanted to know the limits of the golem's strength.

She never noticed I was there until I buried my dagger in her back. The poison worked quickly. As she died, I watched the golem crumble into nothingness. Strange that a such a powerful creature could be brought so low because of its master.

The knife I took from the necromancer was a thing of beauty. It was always cold to the touch, even after holding the blade over an open fire. Runes carved into the weapon matched the symbols I found in her spell books. The bones or flesh of the corpse a necromancer intends to raise are often carved with these same runes. We can use them as well. However, always mark a ward of protection on the ground before using necromancer sigils, for they are powerful things.

Bogan

The superstitious bogans lurk in the Blood Marsh of Westmarch, where they form into small tribes and worship a crude fire deity. They have an extraordinary sense of smell, which makes them expert foragers. Many of the plants they collect—such as elemus leaf and blood moss—are useful for summoning rituals. It is easier to pillage a bogan village for these reagents than to hunt for them in the marsh.

To scare the beasts away, create a small effigy with human hair, moss, and branches from a pine tree. Ignite the object and toss it near the bogans. They will flee in terror, thinking it a sign from their god. I recommend killing a few for extra measure, just to ensure they stay away for a long period of time.

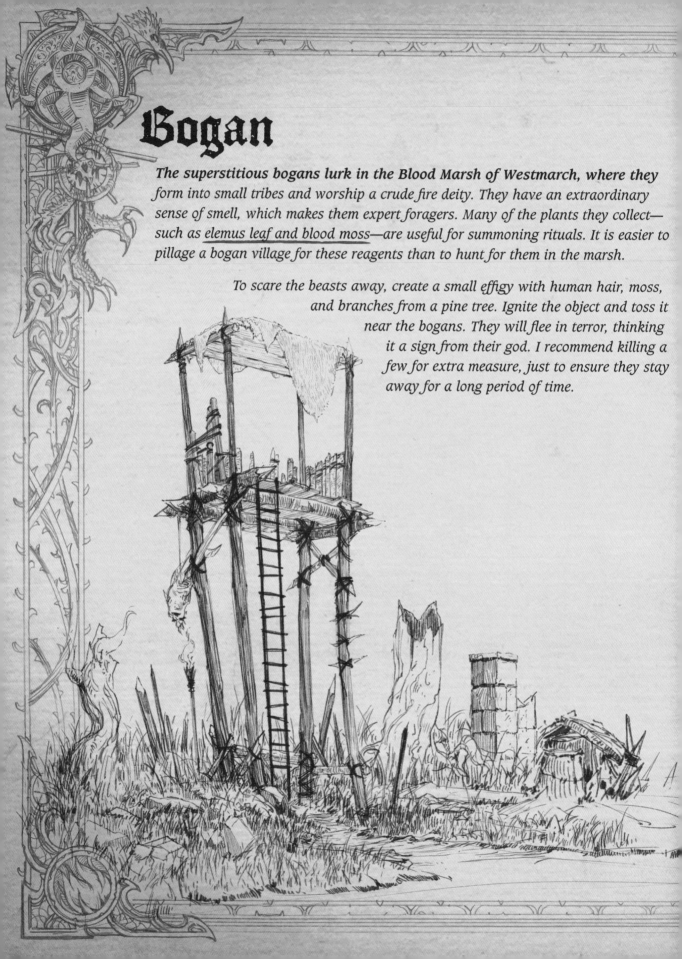

Blood magic suffuses nearly everything in the marsh, including the bogans. Manipulating the region's energy can change the creatures from either more aggressive to more docile.

Scavenger

There are many different types of scavengers. Though they have small physical differences, they are all aggressive and ravenous. Scavengers travel in packs and eat living prey or carrion alike. When food is scarce, they turn on each other. When that is no longer an option they gnaw at their own limbs.

The scavengers may seem like nothing more than pests, but they have some uses. These beasts symbolize ambition and survival. Wearing a scavenger paw the day before important rituals will bring excellent results. However, the paw must be cut from a living scavenger. It cannot be bought or received from another person, or it will lose its power.

Screeching agitates newly summoned demons. Offering them a few scavengers to feed on has a calming effect. This makes it easier to mark the demon's soul or contain it in a circle of entrapment.

Quill Fiend

These vermin are mindless scroungers who are little better than rats. But they are dangerous. Some rarer breeds carry poisons in their quills, while others produce unstable substances that can spontaneously ignite. It is wise to trap rather than kill them so that their bodies can be harvested for any useful reagents later.

Their quills are sturdy and resistant to magic. They can be fashioned into needles for drawing blood and venom from other creatures.

Blood Hawk

I admire the blood hawks. They are patient, clever hunters. They wait until their prey is wounded, distracted, or at some other disadvantage before striking. When they do, it is with all their fury. They hold nothing back.

The Coven can learn from them. It is easy to give in to our passions, to want the full power of the Burning Hells at our fingertips here and now. But there will come a time for that. We must be patient. Be clever hunters. Watch our enemies and learn their weaknesses. And when the Lords of Hell finally command us to strike, we shall do so with all our fury. Holding nothing back.

Blood hawk feathers are resistant to fire and
ice magic, which makes them ideal quills for
writing ritual inscriptions. Pluck a feather from
the middle of the left wing but take only one.
Removing more will dampen its magic properties.

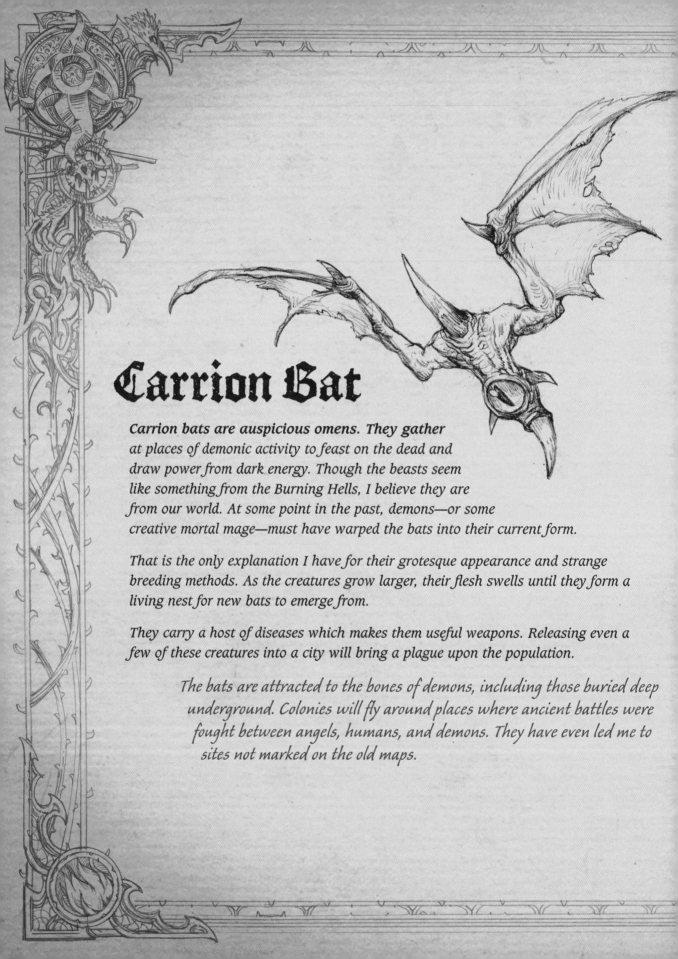

Carrion Bat

Carrion bats are auspicious omens. They gather
at places of demonic activity to feast on the dead and
draw power from dark energy. Though the beasts seem
like something from the Burning Hells, I believe they are
from our world. At some point in the past, demons—or some
creative mortal mage—must have warped the bats into their current form.

That is the only explanation I have for their grotesque appearance and strange
breeding methods. As the creatures grow larger, their flesh swells until they form a
living nest for new bats to emerge from.

They carry a host of diseases which makes them useful weapons. Releasing even a
few of these creatures into a city will bring a plague upon the population.

The bats are attracted to the bones of demons, including those buried deep
underground. Colonies will fly around places where ancient battles were
fought between angels, humans, and demons. They have even led me to
sites not marked on the old maps.

Khazra

Scholars call them "khazra." Children call them "goatmen." In this, the children of Sanctuary know best. They are indeed half goat and half man—just as the foolish Vizjerei intended. But they are not the mindless, loyal weapons the mages wanted to create; they are vicious, cunning, and brutal.

The khazra spent their first generations of life gleefully slaughtering every Vizjerei they could find. Which is what every single mage deserved, as far as I am concerned.

They are distrustful of humans, and rightly so, but since many khazra clans have pledged themselves to demonic masters, they could one day be our allies. And if not, no matter. They retain enough human blood to be adequate for sacrificial rituals.

The khazra shaman and sorcerers are powerful, but beware: They will betray us on a whim. Best to avoid any bargain with them.

Lacuni

I once imagined these feline creatures to be similar to the khazra—wise enough, despite their bestial nature, to know that their destinies lay with the Burning Hells. That is not the case. The lacuni were twisted into panther-like beasts because of their ancestors' foolishness.

Nothing remains in their savage minds but the faintest desire for power, which they will pay any price for. Just as I almost did, once.

A small display of demonic power will dazzle them for a while. They may even pledge themselves to us. Do not trust their loyalty unless their minds are bound with an appropriate spell.

Once subjugated, harvest the eyes of the lacuni. They have many uses. The creatures can see as well at night as they can during the day, and their mystics are gifted scryers.

Cut the eyes from a lacuni with an iron blade, then place them in a box made of reeds and let them dry for a week. To experience visions of the future, draw the symbol of the mystic eye on the ground with lacuni blood, eat one of the beast's eyes, and burn the other eye in an iron pot while inhaling the smoke.

To see better in the dark, coat both eyes in emberlen wax and wear them as a necklace.

Hydra

Hydras are commonly seen in visions. They represent doorways, transformation, and the opening of new paths.

The ancient Triune studied the Zann Esu sorceresses and how they summoned these fiery, multi-headed creatures. At first, the cult believed that the hydras were demons ripped from the Burning Hells, but they were wrong. Hydras are elemental beasts from our own world. They live deep underground near molten veins and pits of fire.

I have seen a hydra in the mystic fires once before. A great beast of many heads, all but one engulfed in flames. The creature never spoke, but it watched me. It peered into me. From the weight of its gaze I know that it holds vast knowledge that will make us stronger.

Spiders

Spiders represent many things: creation, destruction, power, and fear. They are bearers of omens, good and ill. Spotting a spiderweb on the eastern side of trees, bushes, and buildings is a sign of impending hardship.

There are many kinds of spiders in the world, but they all share an affinity for magic. The creatures are sensitive to spells and enchanted artifacts. Over the ages, magic has changed some spiders to expand their minds and create desires that can feel all too human.

The most powerful are known as queens, and they rule over a vast number of lesser creatures. Call them clusters, packs, it does not matter. Just know that they rarely travel alone.

Collect spider silk whenever possible as it is a primary reagent in making paralysis and sleep potions, as well as being good for casting binding and entrapment spells. When harvesting venom, pierce the creature's body once—only once—with a needle to draw out the ichor. Store the venom in a crystal vial for three days before using it to make poisons.

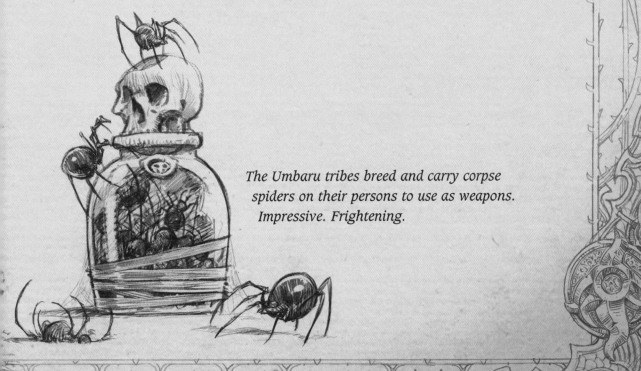

The Umbaru tribes breed and carry corpse spiders on their persons to use as weapons. Impressive. Frightening.

Wood Wraith

These are not trees. Not truly. They began as human spirits who were drawn to the peace of nature, unwilling to move on after death. Some even imagined themselves protectors of their new homes. It takes only a hint of demonic corruption to turn them. Carve a demon lord's symbol into the wraith's trunk and the creature will change almost immediately. A strong hand can then force it to bend all of nature toward the Burning Hells. Quite useful.

Bark harvested from the wraiths contains faint traces of life energies, which make the wood ideal for creating effigies or ritual incense.

For being so small, fetishes are a treasure trove of reagents. The creatures have magic in their bones which gives them various gifts. They have incredible stamina and can travel for days without rest. Dry their hearts and lungs, then grind the organs into a powder for use in potions that grant speed and reflexes.

Fetish

The people of Kurast tell frightening stories of the tiny, human-like fetishes that roam the local jungles. If I did not already know they were native to our world, I would think these creatures were born from the deepest pits of the Hells. The fetishes are individually weak but overcome this flaw with group coordination and deadly weapons. They swarm like rabid dogs, shooting poisoned darts that paralyze their prey so that they can finish the job with their long knives. The bloodthirsty creatures would make fitting servants for a demon lord.

They are susceptible to the influence of demons.
Very susceptible.

Realmwalker

This is not a creature born of Sanctuary, nor of the Burning Hells, or even of the High Heavens.

They come from the chaos of Pandemonium with its endless layering of magics meant for killing, warding, cleansing, and corruption.

Profoundly fascinating, they can shift from one realm to another by instinct alone. Above their heads sit a swirling mass of primal energy that acts as a rift, which allows this effortless travel.

Perhaps we could use one of these creatures to traverse in and out of the Burning Hells with ease. However, their rifts seem unpredictable, so we must be very careful.

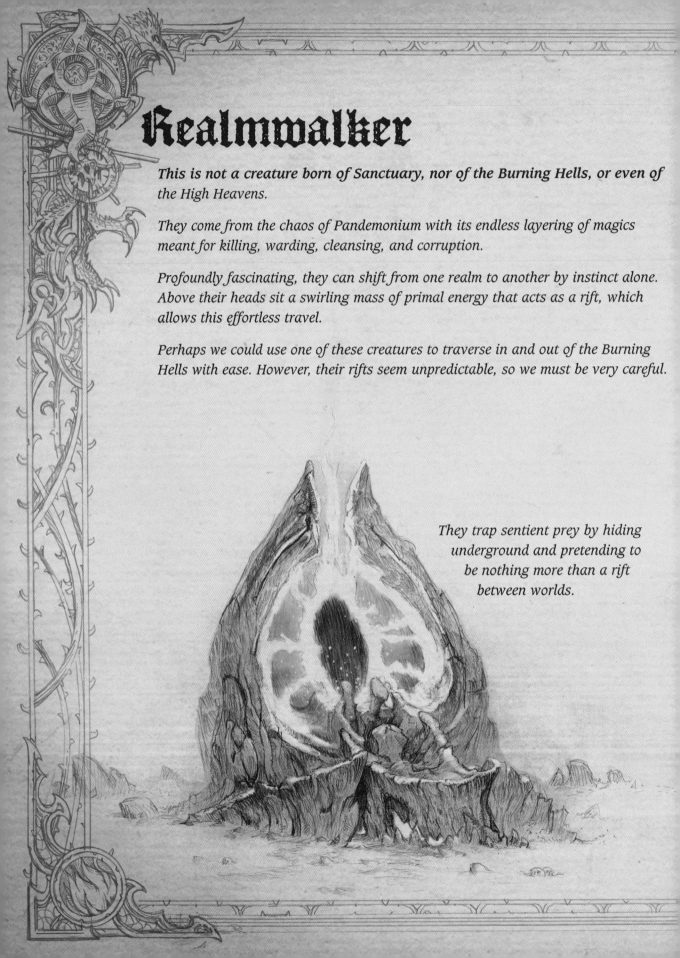

They trap sentient prey by hiding underground and pretending to be nothing more than a rift between worlds.

Scouring Charger

The scouring chargers are attuned to the latent magics of Pandemonium and sustain themselves by feeding off these energies, or the relics discarded by demons and angels. This natural affinity makes these creatures valuable tools for tracking down places of power or harvesting magic.

Follow the creatures from a distance to find areas suffused with energy. Or, kill them and harvest their magic-rich bodies. It makes no difference what method is used. In the end, the results are the same.

The length of a scouring charger's spines is a sign of their age, which determines the amount of magic that can be leeched from their bones. Consider that when choosing which of the beasts to target.

Before I learned of the Black Soulstone, I thought perhaps one of these would be strong enough to contain the essences of the Evils. Alas, the beasts could not.

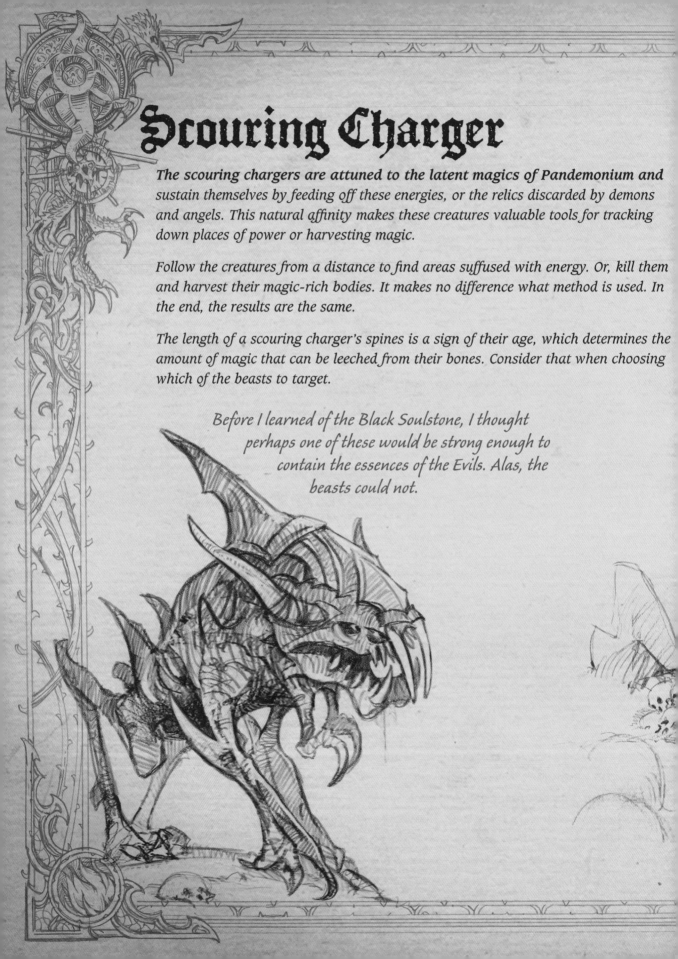

I have traveled many places in search of demon souls to mark. It strikes me how many of these sites I learned about from the old man.

DECKARD CAIN is a wanderer and a scholar, but now he serves simply as the vessel's guardian.

He adopted the girl and is teaching her the ancient histories. He must see her as a student of sorts. Someone to carry on his work after he is gone.

Age is taking its toll on him, but he still has that spark of hope. The same I saw in Tristram when we first met. He was as lonely a man then as he is now. Always lost in his books. Always looking for his purpose by digging through the past.

A man who doesn't know himself is too eager to trust. He will cling to anyone with confidence because he believes they have the answers he needs. It was easy to make Cain believe I came to Tristram to stop Diablo. I shared what I knew of demons, and he offered me stories about the Horadrim, Kulle, and other subjects in return.

We both gained something from our time together. He gave me the knowledge I needed. I gave him a destiny, whether he knew it or not.

He will care for the vessel and keep her safe until I have drawn the Evils into the Black Soulstone.

The Angels of the High Heavens

It is the angels that I see as the most dangerous to humanity. They hunt and eliminate any source of disorder, and they think themselves brave and honorable for it. Sanctuary has only avoided an invasion from the High Heavens because perhaps—perhaps!—we will not side against them.

This is not an act of compassion. It is a threat. A leash.

If humanity ever forges its own destiny—or finds its fate alongside the Burning Hells—we will all find ourselves burning in "holy" fire.

That is why we must know these creatures, for we will one day face them in battle.

Angiris Council

High in the clouds lies a paradise. A silver city of hope. All the angels that walk its streets are shining paragons of heroism who always know what is right, and always fight in the name of peace and decency. Such are the tales told to children.

A brief glimpse of the Eternal Conflict makes lies of all those stories. Angels and Demons both make war because it is in their nature. Very few on either side have any true insight into their own destinies. They fight because they were born to fight. They corrupt because they are corrupted. They make order out of chaos because they know no other path.

Once I discovered the power and the possibilities of the dark arts, my mind began to despise the creatures of the High Heavens. The darkest part of my heart was reserved for their leaders, the Angiris Council. It was a reflexive hatred, but the more I learn, the more it fades.

Angels are not innately deserving of my hatred. You cannot blame any creature for their nature, only for their choices. Angels are born with the purpose of bringing order to existence. It must be a curse to have such a false, impossible, self-contradicting goal. Only a few in the entire history of the Eternal Conflict—on either side— have ever questioned their purpose, and fewer still have acted upon it.

I have seen into their hearts through the eyes of the few demons who have witnessed their acts in the Eternal Conflict. I know them thusly:

Imperius, the Archangel of Valor—*A creature that kills indiscriminately with the unshakable belief that his cause is just.*

Auriel, the Archangel of Hope—*Optimism is a strange luxury for combatants in the Eternal Conflict, and not one that Sanctuary should ever indulge.*

Itherael, the Archangel of Fate—*This one can see the future of angels and demons, but not of humanity. Little wonder why the Burning Hells prize us so.*

Malthael, the Archangel of Wisdom—*The one mind on the Council that questions the nature of their existence and the implications of their war. But his answers only lead him to more conflict.*

Tyrael, the Archangel of Justice—*Be wary of this one. Of all the Angiris Council, only he has directly intervened on Sanctuary. According to Horadrim tomes, he formed their ancient order centuries ago. I've found no sign that he would confront us directly, but he will certainly aid our enemies with information and power.*

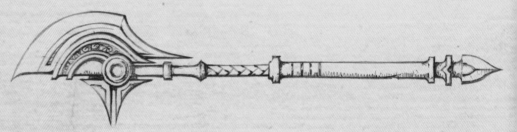

Fortunately for us, the angelic hosts have agreed to leave Sanctuary to its own fate. For now. Several angels have broken that agreement, but they were forced to do so cautiously and invisibly, or else face judgment from the Council. This is fine, but we must act carefully if we are to walk where angels tread.

As creatures of order, they will oppose us at every opportunity.

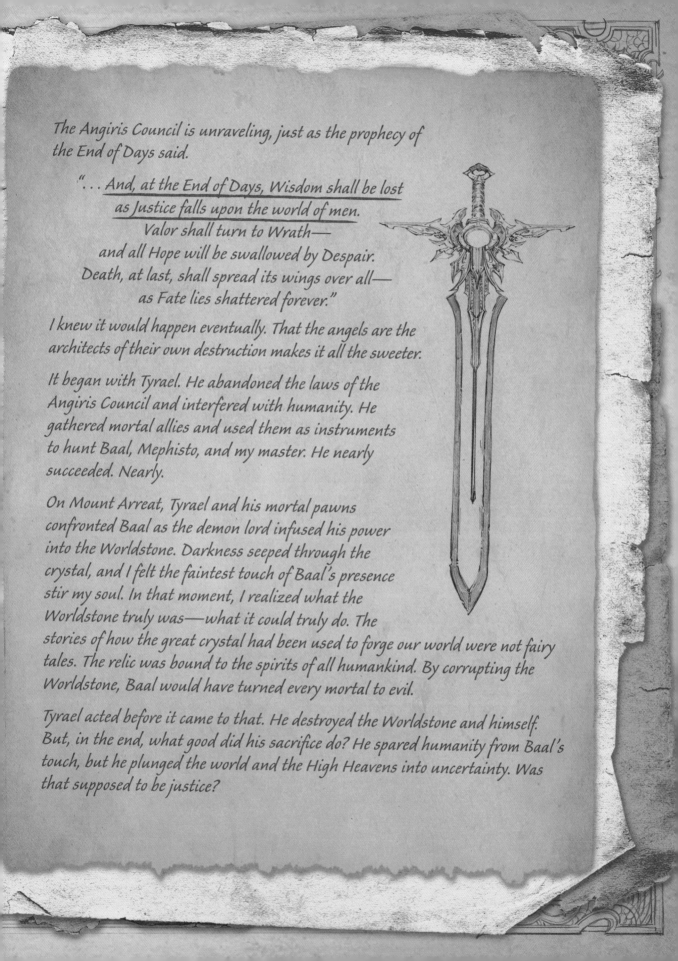

The Angiris Council is unraveling, just as the prophecy of the End of Days said.

"... <u>And, at the End of Days, Wisdom shall be lost</u>
<u>as Justice falls upon the world of men.</u>
Valor shall turn to Wrath—
and all Hope will be swallowed by Despair.
Death, at last, shall spread its wings over all—
as Fate lies shattered forever."

I knew it would happen eventually. That the angels are the architects of their own destruction makes it all the sweeter.

It began with Tyrael. He abandoned the laws of the Angiris Council and interfered with humanity. He gathered mortal allies and used them as instruments to hunt Baal, Mephisto, and my master. He nearly succeeded. Nearly.

On Mount Arreat, Tyrael and his mortal pawns confronted Baal as the demon lord infused his power into the Worldstone. Darkness seeped through the crystal, and I felt the faintest touch of Baal's presence stir my soul. In that moment, I realized what the Worldstone truly was—what it could truly do. The stories of how the great crystal had been used to forge our world were not fairy tales. The relic was bound to the spirits of all humankind. By corrupting the Worldstone, Baal would have turned every mortal to evil.

Tyrael acted before it came to that. He destroyed the Worldstone and himself. But, in the end, what good did his sacrifice do? He spared humanity from Baal's touch, but he plunged the world and the High Heavens into uncertainty. Was that supposed to be justice?

MALTHAEL was the next to break from the Angiris Council. The Worldstone's destruction did something to him. He disappeared from the High Heavens. Did he know what Tyrael had done and why? Perhaps he did, and then realized that no matter what the angels did, the demons would eventually find a way to control humanity. Perhaps that was his last, and most profound, gasp of wisdom. He knew that the Angiris Council's quest to preserve order was unattainable, and he abandoned it.

For that, at least, he has my respect. He is not a fool like the other angels, but that makes him unpredictable. Unknowable. Dangerous.

I have seen visions of him in Pandemonium, lost in contemplation. He is searching for something. The calmness that once shrouded him is gone and replaced with a dark new power. It radiates off him, even in my visions. A wave of icy black surging over me, stabbing at my spirit like a thousand needles. Like me, he has taken a path to power. One from which there is no going back.

Without him and Tyrael—without wisdom and justice—what hope does the Angiris Council stand against the Burning Hells?

Malthael's servants are looking for him, but those who find the archangel in Pandemonium never return to the Heavens. They cast away wisdom and gather in his shadow.

Many are the angelic **MAIDENS** who tended Malthael's Pools of Wisdom. They once sang refrains that could draw anyone into a deep trance and reveal insights and visions.

Now they are silent. Do they still have the powers they once did? If I could capture their voices, could they show me what I wish to see?

The maidens are not the only angels who have left the Heavens. Malthael's **ANARCHS** are in Pandemonium as well.

They represented the balance Malthael brought to the Angiris Council. Each of their arms stood for one of the Archangels, with the sixth symbolizing the order and harmony that bound them together. Anyone standing near them experienced calm introspection.

Now their ethereal bodies are gone and instead replaced with twisted flesh. A dark aura washes over any creature who gets too close to them. When time permits, I must study them more. Their skin holds potent magic. Perhaps a poison of some kind.

The Demons of the Burning Hells

The Coven made a pact long ago that each of us is bound to. All must obey the Lord of Terror, the Lord of Destruction, and the Lord of Hatred in every way, even unto death.

So I state clearly, for those who have forgotten: we serve only them. We do not serve all the Burning Hells. We are not bound to the Lesser Evils, nor must we bow before any demon that crosses our path.

We are not slaves. We are wondrous creatures. That is why the Burning Hells seek our power. We will one day tip the balance of the Eternal Conflict, and reap rewards beyond that of any other human. We bargained for our destinies. We owe nothing less than our freely given souls.

And if we fail, we deserve our fates.

Only when the Eternal Conflict ends shall our rewards come due. Some of us will be raised to serve at the right hands of the Lords of Hell. Some will be lifted above the Lesser Evils. And some will even rule Sanctuary and the other worlds.

But only those who demonstrate their worthiness will receive such honor. The weak will not be raised above the strong. The confident shall not supplant the capable. We will rise as far as our strength allows us and not an inch further.

Do not whisper about the fairness of this agreement. The minions of the Burning Hells do not deal in "fair." They deal in strength.

Strength comes through cunning and knowledge. Treat the denizens of the Burning Hells as if they were any creature on Sanctuary. Learn how to use their power, else be in their servitude on the final day of the Eternal Conflict.

Cydaea, the Maiden of Lust

To see three spiders on the same web is a sign that Cydaea or her minions are near. Dreams of passion will follow. Do not indulge in these visions, for they will lead to an unpleasant fate.

A Kehjistani mystic once saw the face of Cydaea. He described her as a demon of extremes, half beautiful goddess, and half nightmarish spider. The mystic claimed the sound of her voice was like music that lulled him into a state of euphoria before he realized she was speaking of feeding his body parts to her spiderlings.

After coming out of his vision, the mystic swore to never look on such a revolting creature again. It only took a few days to break his vow. He entered a trance to see Cydaea again, but never woke from it. Before he died, his fellow mystics described his face as constantly shifting between pleasure, pain, lust, and revulsion.

She is the most favored of Azmodan's seven sin lieutenants. I imagine that for her to achieve such a standing her powers must have some effect on the Lord of Sin.

Cydaea is often attended by swarms of spiderlings and her favored, the winged succubi.

Deceiver

The deceivers could be anyone. A merchant in Lut Gholein. A beggar in the back alleys of Caldeum. A servant in Westmarch's royal court. That is their strength: to shroud their forms and get close to their enemies. Only when they are ready to strike will their illusion fade, and their true, serpentine form appear. This mastery of deception is a gift from Belial, the Lord of Lies, and it makes the deceivers feared even by other demons.

To harness the power of a deceiver's scale, place it on a level surface and mark a circle around it with Ammuit illusion runes. Invoke the name of Belial until the scale shimmers and becomes barely visible. Then bind it in an amulet. This object will shroud whoever wears it in an illusion.

A powerful tool. It has allowed me to go many places unseen.
Even the Ammuit mages, the masters of illusion, have difficulties
sensing my glamour.

Armored Destroyer

The Vizjerei call these creatures the kalutan, while the Triune simply refer to them as the armored destroyers. I would not call them servants or even soldiers of Diablo. The writings of the Vizjerei portray them more like an infestation. They swarm across the Lord of Terror's realm taking flight on sharp-edged wings or scrabbling up cliffs and into chasms with their hooked claws. As the Vizjerei once learned, they are just as dangerous in the air as they are on the ground.

One of the clan's mages thought the armored destroyers were weak. He thought that since there were many of them it would not be difficult to summon only one to bend to his will. After being brought over, the destroyer broke free from the mage's control and cut him in half with a single swipe of its wing. It took a handful of Vizjerei to finally contain the demon. Not all of them survived.

That was only one destroyer. Imagine what an army of them could do to this world.

I summoned an armored destroyer in order to experiment with marking its spirit. The demon must have sensed we serve the same master, for as it drew near, it lowered its head in obedience.

The Butcher

Accounts from Vizjerei mages tell of the Butcher, a creature constructed from the body parts of other demons. An arm from here. An eye from there. This was done for reasons beyond sadism. The Butcher gained the strength and power of the different demons that were a part of it. This makes the patchwork creatures extremely powerful, but also extremely bloodthirsty.

The Vizjerei wrote that urges to tear, dismember, and consume constantly drove the Butcher to commit new acts of violence. Perhaps that was a product of its unique creation, or perhaps it just enjoyed inflicting pain.

Whether the Butcher still exists or not is a mystery, but stories about it have persisted throughout the years. Even in recent times, I have heard of demonologists trying to make creatures similar to the Butcher.

Blood magic is needed to bind the parts together. It is best to start with a head or a heart. Use stitches made from lacuni hair and wait one day between fusing each of the other body parts together.

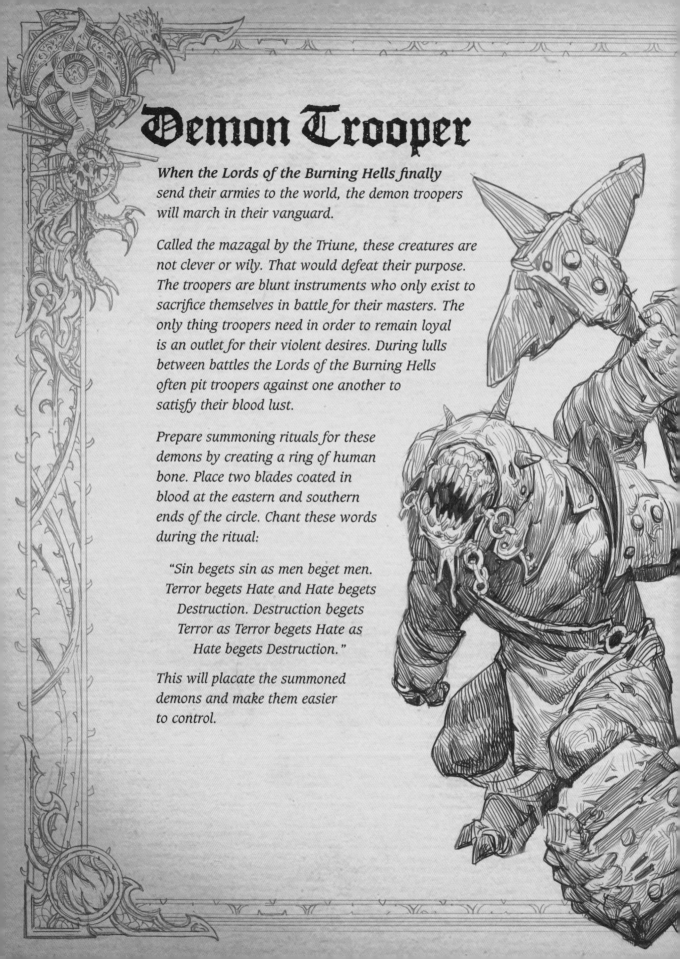

Demon Trooper

When the Lords of the Burning Hells finally send their armies to the world, the demon troopers will march in their vanguard.

Called the mazagal by the Triune, these creatures are not clever or wily. That would defeat their purpose. The troopers are blunt instruments who only exist to sacrifice themselves in battle for their masters. The only thing troopers need in order to remain loyal is an outlet for their violent desires. During lulls between battles the Lords of the Burning Hells often pit troopers against one another to satisfy their blood lust.

Prepare summoning rituals for these demons by creating a ring of human bone. Place two blades coated in blood at the eastern and southern ends of the circle. Chant these words during the ritual:

"Sin begets sin as men beget men. Terror begets Hate and Hate begets Destruction. Destruction begets Terror as Terror begets Hate as Hate begets Destruction."

This will placate the summoned demons and make them easier to control.

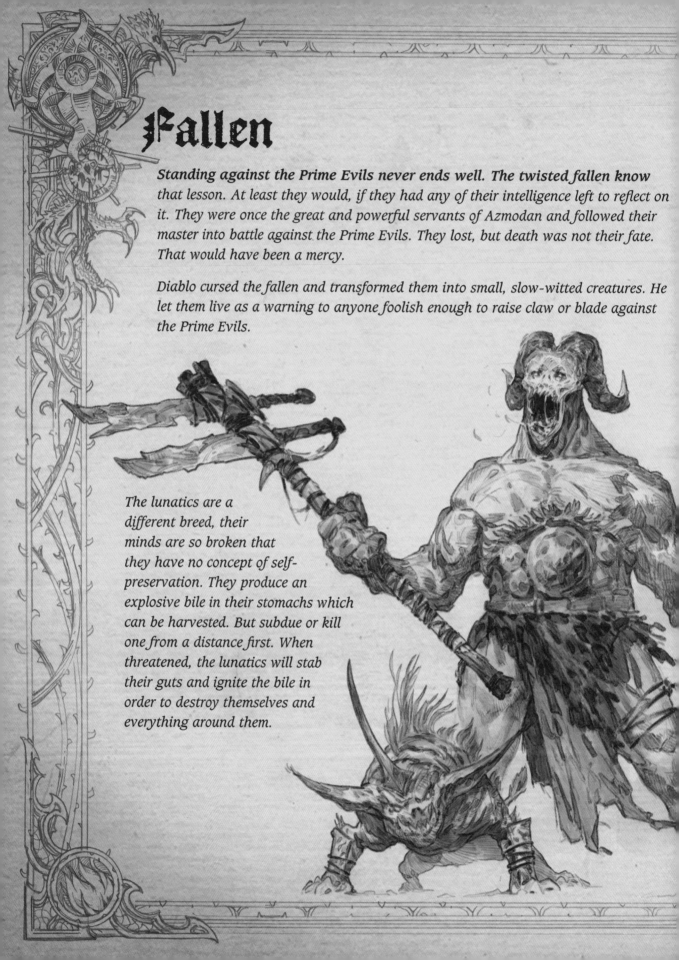

Fallen

Standing against the Prime Evils never ends well. The twisted fallen know that lesson. At least they would, if they had any of their intelligence left to reflect on it. They were once the great and powerful servants of Azmodan and followed their master into battle against the Prime Evils. They lost, but death was not their fate. That would have been a mercy.

Diablo cursed the fallen and transformed them into small, slow-witted creatures. He let them live as a warning to anyone foolish enough to raise claw or blade against the Prime Evils.

The lunatics are a different breed, their minds are so broken that they have no concept of self-preservation. They produce an explosive bile in their stomachs which can be harvested. But subdue or kill one from a distance first. When threatened, the lunatics will stab their guts and ignite the bile in order to destroy themselves and everything around them.

The fallen are crude, but they do observe a simple hierarchy.
The shaman priests are at the top. They have some command
over magic, and they are able to animate dead fallen in the
heat of battle. These powers are enough
to earn the fear and respect of their kind.
Even the much larger, brutish
overseers obey the will of
the shaman.

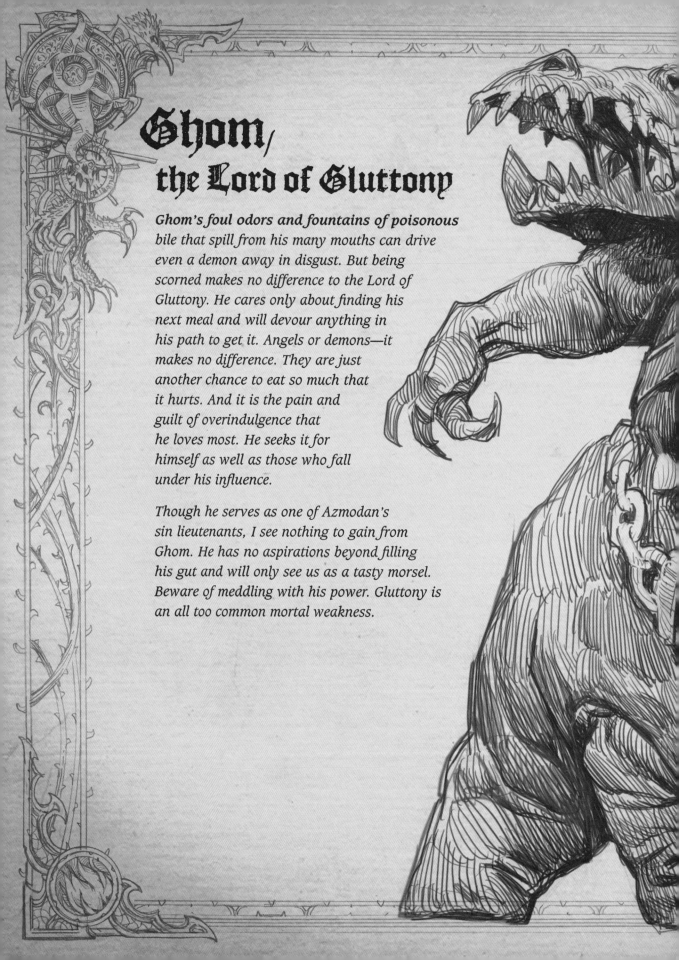

Ghom,
the Lord of Gluttony

Ghom's foul odors and fountains of poisonous bile that spill from his many mouths can drive even a demon away in disgust. But being scorned makes no difference to the Lord of Gluttony. He cares only about finding his next meal and will devour anything in his path to get it. Angels or demons—it makes no difference. They are just another chance to eat so much that it hurts. And it is the pain and guilt of overindulgence that he loves most. He seeks it for himself as well as those who fall under his influence.

Though he serves as one of Azmodan's sin lieutenants, I see nothing to gain from Ghom. He has no aspirations beyond filling his gut and will only see us as a tasty morsel. Beware of meddling with his power. Gluttony is an all too common mortal weakness.

Hellion

The hellions are the hounds of the Burning Hells. They are swift, tireless, and can outrun almost any creature on Sanctuary. The hellions are not clever demons, but we do not need them to be for our purposes. Because of their simple minds they are easy to summon from the Hells. Fear and pain will break them into loyal servants. In that way, they are not much different than men.

But we must never turn our backs on a hellion. As loyal as we may think they might be, they are still demons. And they will take any chance they can to destroy us.

Hellions are excellent weapons and sources for reagents. Grind their claws, teeth, and horns into a powder, then ingest with water to induce visions of the place in the Hells where they came from. Preserve and shrink their hearts or heads and place them around the necks of risen dead to make the creatures more obedient.

Shadow Vermin

I have seen the shadow vermin in my dreams. They rushed in around me in a tide of inky black that reflected no light. Long arms and narrow faces rose from the darkness. They went up around my legs, then over my chest. I screamed in terror as they filled my throat and blinded my eyes, but when I stopped fighting a calm washed over me.

The darkness was pleasant. I felt whole as I floated through it.

These demons are a concentration of Diablo's power. They are the fears of all humankind made manifest. If we fight them, we will succumb to terror. But if we embrace them, we will never know fear again, because we are one with it.

Herald of Pestilence

The heralds of pestilence were not always twisted and plague-ridden. They were turned after launching a failed insurrection against Azmodan. The Lord of Sin punished the demons by changing one of their arms into a long insect-like limb infused with poison. The substance was so strong that it disfigured the heralds and made them into living vessels of plagues and diseases.

As much as the demons hated what had been done to them, they could never take vengeance against Azmodan. The Lord of Sin made himself immune to their poison. That was his real punishment: to give the heralds a weapon so powerful it could kill anything except the one demon they truly wanted to destroy.

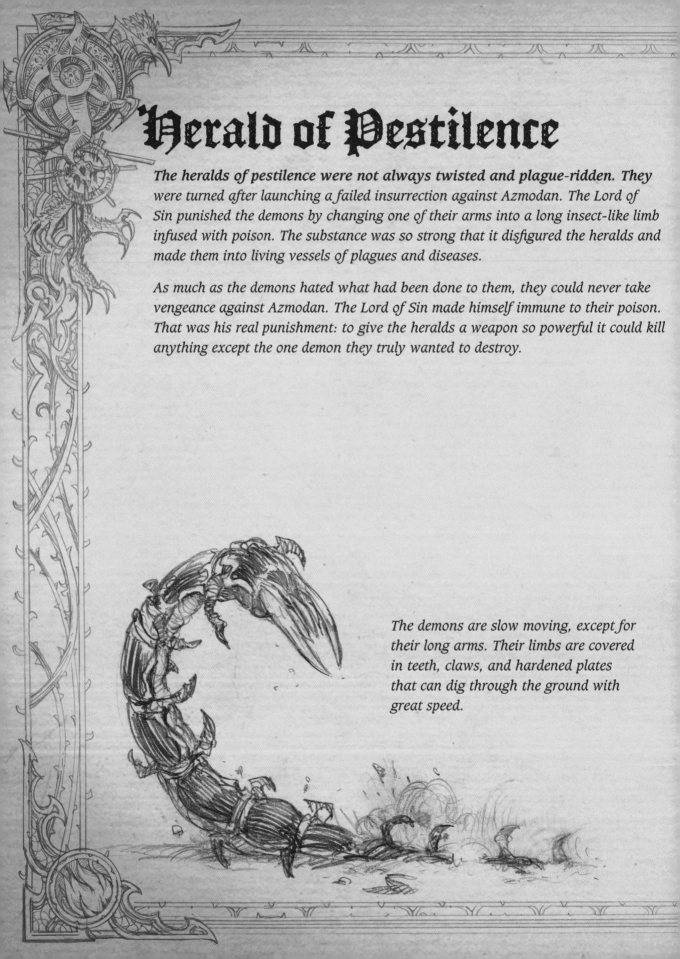

The demons are slow moving, except for their long arms. Their limbs are covered in teeth, claws, and hardened plates that can dig through the ground with great speed.

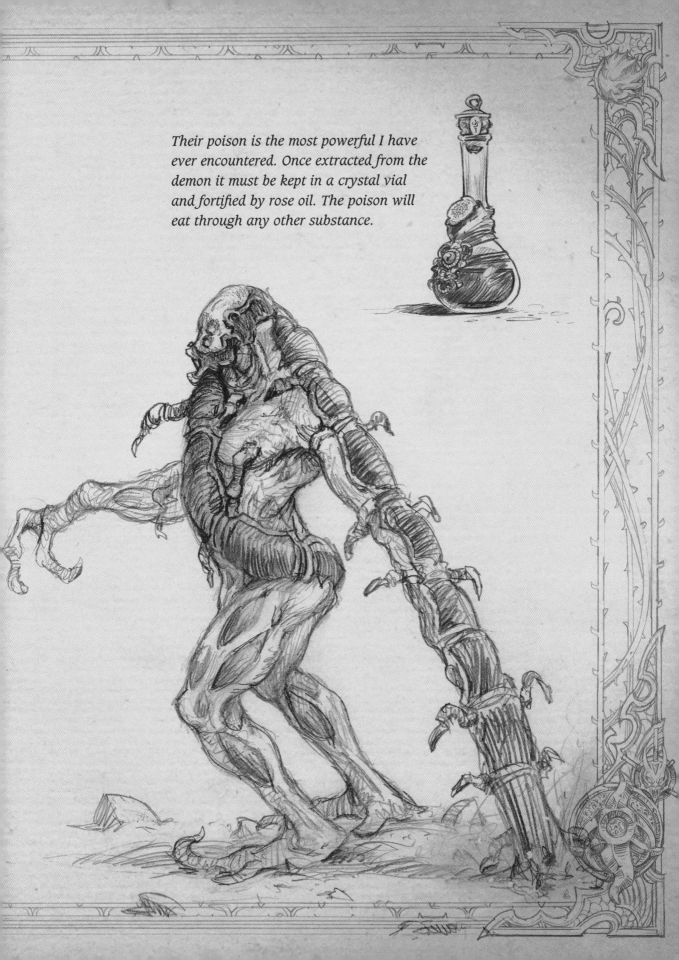

Their poison is the most powerful I have ever encountered. Once extracted from the demon it must be kept in a crystal vial and fortified by rose oil. The poison will eat through any other substance.

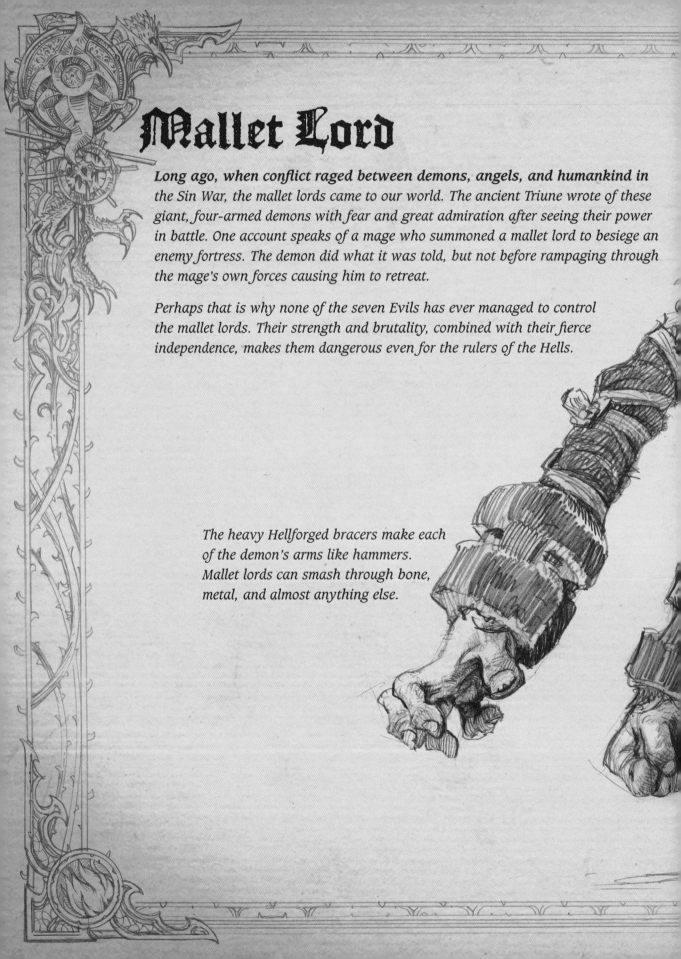

Mallet Lord

Long ago, when conflict raged between demons, angels, and humankind in the Sin War, the mallet lords came to our world. The ancient Triune wrote of these giant, four-armed demons with fear and great admiration after seeing their power in battle. One account speaks of a mage who summoned a mallet lord to besiege an enemy fortress. The demon did what it was told, but not before rampaging through the mage's own forces causing him to retreat.

Perhaps that is why none of the seven Evils has ever managed to control the mallet lords. Their strength and brutality, combined with their fierce independence, makes them dangerous even for the rulers of the Hells.

The heavy Hellforged bracers make each of the demon's arms like hammers. Mallet lords can smash through bone, metal, and almost anything else.

Morlu

History is filled with tales of great warriors who were pure of heart and mind. They are all lies. These so-called heroes were like everyone else. They had weaknesses and fears. They had dark secrets and even darker regrets. These flaws are what Mephisto, Lord of Hatred, used to twist many heroic warriors into bloodthirsty creatures called the morlu.

During the Sin War, the morlu served as tireless weapons in the Triune's military. Not even death could stop them. Morlu who fell in battle were resurrected by the Triune to fight again. These warriors learned from their mistakes in previous battles. Each time they came back to life, they were deadlier and more experienced than before.

I do not know what became of the morlu after the Sin War, but I am certain they found a place in the Hells. They are too valuable a weapon to abandon.

We serve the same master now.

Diablo has gifted the morlu with even greater power.

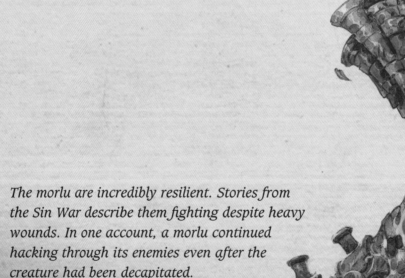

The morlu are incredibly resilient. Stories from the Sin War describe them fighting despite heavy wounds. In one account, a morlu continued hacking through its enemies even after the creature had been decapitated.

Oppressor

It is said the fire burning inside the oppressors—or "zashari" as they were called by ancient demonologists—is the breath of their creator: Baal, Lord of Destruction. He made them as a smith would forge a weapon, infusing the demons with some of his power and transforming them into killing machines. I cannot argue with the results. Every account of the oppressors describes them as the perfect soldiers. The Hellforged weapons they wield can shatter bones and armor with ease, but the demons can just as easily tear an enemy apart with their hands.

If the stories of their origins are true, it might seem ironic that Baal made these demons, let alone anything at all. But he has been known to create for the purpose of destruction. That is why his realm is home to the Hellforge, where the most powerful weapons are made.

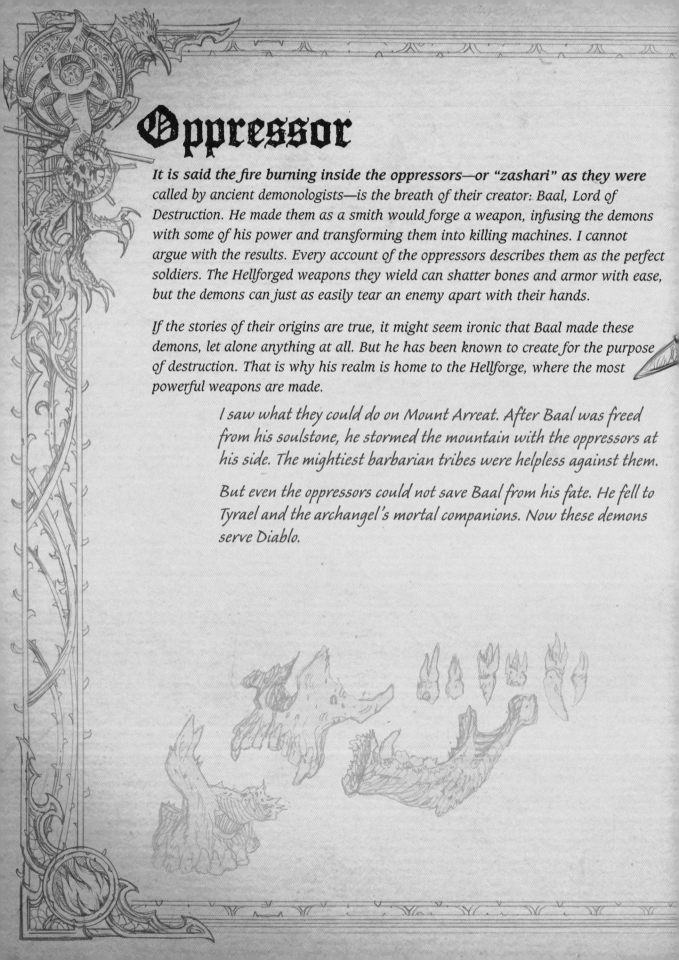

I saw what they could do on Mount Arreat. After Baal was freed from his soulstone, he stormed the mountain with the oppressors at his side. The mightiest barbarian tribes were helpless against them.

But even the oppressors could not save Baal from his fate. He fell to Tyrael and the archangel's mortal companions. Now these demons serve Diablo.

Sand Dweller

The ancient Vizjerei might have been short-sighted and foolish, but they were talented summoners. Many of the demons they brought to our world are still here, including the sand dwellers. The Vizjerei named these creatures the haz'jareen, meaning "branded ones." They marked the sand dwellers with control runes and commanded the demons to guard their vaults and estates. Which the monsters did, even long after their masters died. Time and the elements turned the demons' hides into thick, craggy, stone-like skin but they still wander areas like the Desolate Sands, where the Vizjerei first set them on their eternal watch.

Even after all these years, the control runes branded on the demons remain active. Three people must be present to alter the runes and bring the guardian under control. One must chant the Vizjerei commandments of servitude. Another must write the demon's control rune on human flesh, preferably their own. And last, one person must—while these other activities are underway—strike the guardian's rune with an amethyst wand.

Zoltun Kulle was obsessed with the sand dwellers. He found a way to exert his will over the creatures and commanded them to guard his hidden vaults and libraries beneath the desert.

Siegebreaker

The siegebreakers are few, but even one can turn the tide of battle. The Evils used them to great effect when breaching the defenses of Pandemonium Fortress while it was held by the angels. But as with all things, such power comes at a price. Siegebreakers can by unruly, even when commanded by the Prime Evils. The Triune learned this lesson the hard way when they summoned the creatures in the Sin War. They tried to bind the monstrous demons in enchanted shackles, but nothing could secure the creatures. The siegebreakers brought the walls of the Triune's summoning chambers crashing down.

Is that kind of destruction worth the cost? I believe it is.

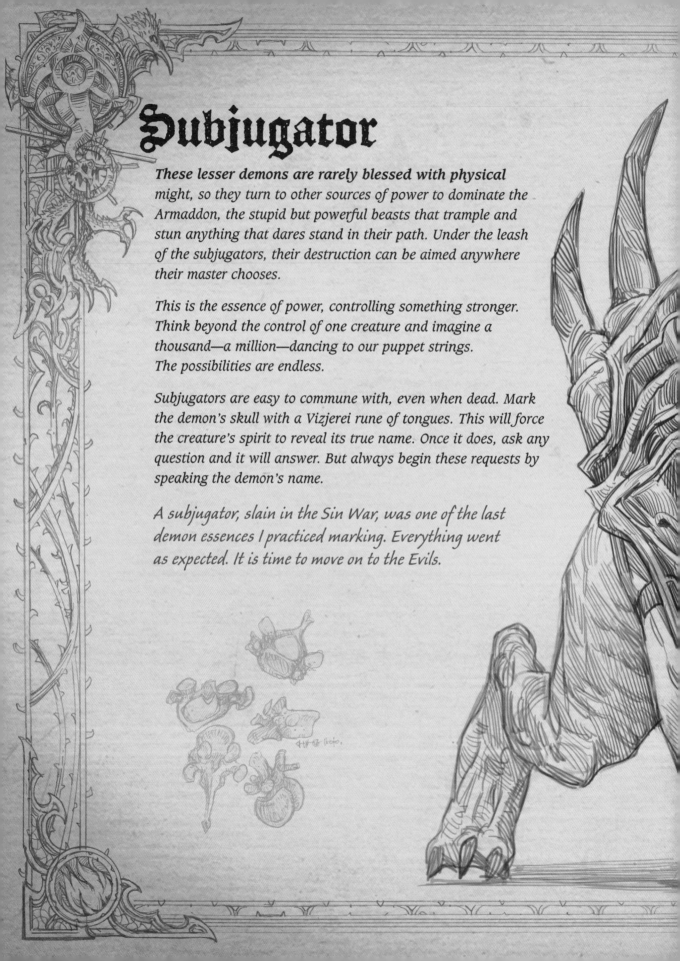

Subjugator

These lesser demons are rarely blessed with physical might, so they turn to other sources of power to dominate the Armaddon, the stupid but powerful beasts that trample and stun anything that dares stand in their path. Under the leash of the subjugators, their destruction can be aimed anywhere their master chooses.

This is the essence of power, controlling something stronger. Think beyond the control of one creature and imagine a thousand—a million—dancing to our puppet strings. The possibilities are endless.

Subjugators are easy to commune with, even when dead. Mark the demon's skull with a Vizjerei rune of tongues. This will force the creature's spirit to reveal its true name. Once it does, ask any question and it will answer. But always begin these requests by speaking the demon's name.

A subjugator, slain in the Sin War, was one of the last demon essences I practiced marking. Everything went as expected. It is time to move on to the Evils.

Succubus

There are legends of women dressed in scarlet, dancing through the forests at night or in the dark alleys of city streets. To see them means that the succubi are hunting their next victim.

Azmodan may have perfected their use, but I believe Andariel, the Maiden of Anguish, was the first to sculpt her demons into these beautiful forms. She was quite clever to teach her minions the art of seduction. Temptation is so powerful a force that one might believe it is its own form of magic.

Many succubi will warn their victims about their true heritage before they strike: a glimpse of demonic wings, a hint of sharpened teeth, a flash of a forked tongue—anything that will seem dangerous to the humans of Sanctuary. The men and women rarely flee. Lust may be the succubi's weapon, but it is the thought of tasting something forbidden that truly ensnares their victims. The allure of pleasures beyond mortal flesh is a sweet honey that drowns out the bitterness of caution.

That allure permeates the succubi's flesh. Wearing bits of the demon's wings, teeth, and other body parts as jewelry will make it easy to seduce anyone.

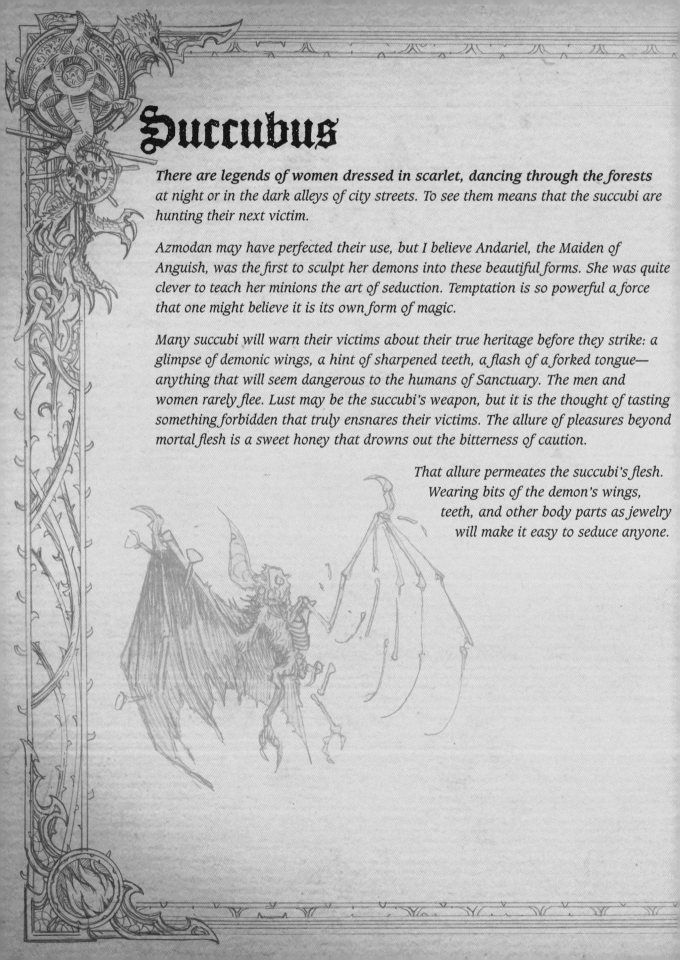

Treasure Goblin

Old stories refer to these creatures as the Drunkard's Faerie because people dumbfounded with drink often see a small creature carrying a bag of gold out of the corner of their eye. Many historians believe they are a race of goblins that are native to our world, but that is not the case. They are demons.

I confess that I once thought these creatures were worth hunting. The moment I saw the gold and jewels they carried upon their backs, I felt the pull of greed. I spent weeks seeking their treasures for my own. That is the trap. These goblins are minions of Greed, a powerful demon lord, who lures selfish and covetous adventurers to their doom in a sea of riches they will never spend.

But it matters little. This demon lord has no ambition beyond her hoard. I say let her wallow in it. We seek another destiny.

Andariel,
The Maiden of Anguish

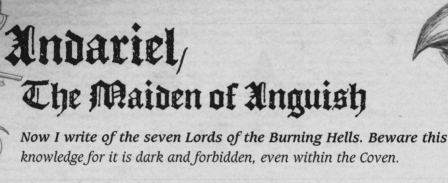

Now I write of the seven Lords of the Burning Hells. Beware this knowledge for it is dark and forbidden, even within the Coven.

I know what the scholars say of the demon lords' beginnings. For once, the secret histories of the Vizjerei, the sealed tomes of Ivgorod, and the texts of the old Triune agree: each of the Evils were spawned from the seven heads of Tathamet, the first being to challenge the eternal order of Anu.

I do not care of their ancient origins, only their final purpose.

Andariel is a frightening creature. She desires, more than anything, to inflict horrors that crack open the minds of her victims. Pain is her tool, not her end. Daggers can kill, but anguish lingers on and eats away at the mind, reducing its prey to nothing.

Others within the Coven have attempted to seek her favor, but none have ever been seen again. I once encountered a beautiful maiden who tempted me with promises of power. The whispers in my dreams told me she was lying, so I refused.

Andariel is ambitious, cunning, and dangerous, but she moves in the shadows and latches onto the plans of the other demon lords as she sees fit. My dreams tell me that her fate will not be her own, but one chosen by someone more powerful.

I believe the Coven should never make treaty with her. If we must enter the service of the Burning Hells, we must do so in the service of the one who shall reign supreme.

Duriel, Lord of Pain

The Lord of Pain is perhaps the simplest of the Great Evils to understand. None in the Coven dream of seeking his power or patronage, not even for the most selfish of reasons. Duriel has no desire or ambition beyond inflicting pain. What could we offer him, save to volunteer our time in his care? Whereas Andariel relishes the anticipation of pain and the fear it creates, Duriel only cares of the existence and propagation of agony.

He is clever, yes. He always seeks new avenues of torment and new victims to flay. This has made him easy to control. The Prime Evils, Belial, and others have enticed him to do their bidding simply by promising him a fresh symphony of screaming to enjoy.

Perhaps we could entice him in the same way. Not by offering servitude, but by offering whole villages and towns up for his sadistic needs.

Communing with Duriel or his minions requires a payment of pain. Only in the throes of agony can these demons be contacted. Self-inflicted wounds caused by whipping or branding are ideal methods for this.

Andariel was the first I marked for the Black Soulstone. The ritual was quick, just as my master promised it would be. I confess, I find it strange that the soul of one of the mightiest creatures in existence could be manipulated with such a simple pattern. Yet, it is comforting. I have been chosen because I am capable of this. The Maiden of Anguish is the first proof of my ultimate victory.

Subduing anguish is like bottling poison. Without the right container, the toxic fluids would eat at the walls and spill out.

For this ritual: Encircle four infinity knots woven from khazra hair with the leaves of any evergreen tree. Each knot should be connected by drippings of human blood.

It went as planned. But I did not expect Andariel to watch me. She looked into my soul as I worked to subdue hers, and for a moment, I witnessed her surprise. She realized my intentions and fought as hard as she could. If she had been fully formed, she would have defeated me.

But she was not.

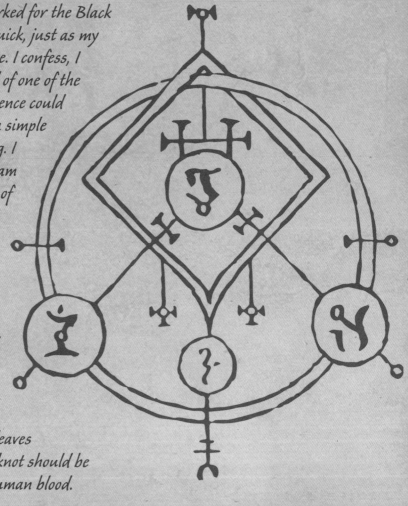

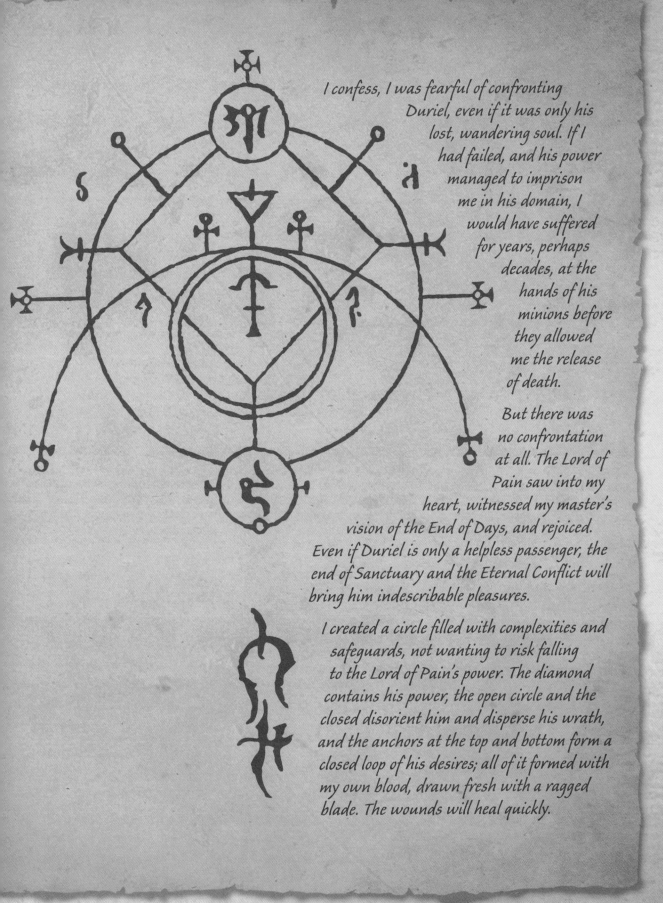

I confess, I was fearful of confronting Duriel, even if it was only his lost, wandering soul. If I had failed, and his power managed to imprison me in his domain, I would have suffered for years, perhaps decades, at the hands of his minions before they allowed me the release of death.

But there was no confrontation at all. The Lord of Pain saw into my heart, witnessed my master's vision of the End of Days, and rejoiced. Even if Duriel is only a helpless passenger, the end of Sanctuary and the Eternal Conflict will bring him indescribable pleasures.

I created a circle filled with complexities and safeguards, not wanting to risk falling to the Lord of Pain's power. The diamond contains his power, the open circle and the closed disorient him and disperse his wrath, and the anchors at the top and bottom form a closed loop of his desires; all of it formed with my own blood, drawn fresh with a ragged blade. The wounds will heal quickly.

Azmodan, The Lord of Sin

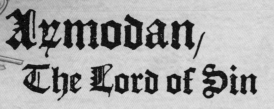

I have learned that many powerful demon lords are trapped here on Sanctuary. In their absence, the Lesser Evils have rushed to fill the void of power and have battled each other for dominance. The Lord of Sin has been the most successful in that war.

Azmodan knows the glory of power and the sweetness of sin. He knows that pleasure is a weapon and ambition is a vulnerability. It is fitting that he is consumed by his own ambition. He chafed when the Prime Evils held sway over him and wants nothing more than to subjugate and control all the realms of Hell.

I believe he could succeed. But I also believe he must not. Sanctuary and humanity mean less than nothing to him. Azmodan's victory would see humanity erased, used for nothing more than fleeting pleasures.

It may be arrogance, but I believe we are more than that.

And I finally found a master that agrees.

If the need arises to deal with Azmodan, or his servants, be sure to fast for at least three days beforehand. This will clear the mind of all desire and make it easier to resist the Lord of Sin's influence.

Belial,
The Lord of Lies

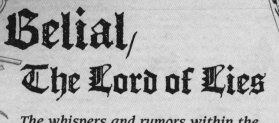

The whispers and rumors within the Coven have filled me with hope and fear in equal numbers. Many of us believe that we have already made contact with a Prime Evil of the Burning Hells. Our predecessors in the Triune served them during the Sin Wars, so we assume it is one of them. This may be so, but I doubt it. The Prime Evils are imprisoned on this world, unable to act freely.

Or so I thought. Diablo's influence was strong enough to reach out to me—and others— from his prison.

If it is not them, who else is it? Which of the Lesser Evils would relish deceiving even us, his loyal followers? Who else but Belial, the Lord of Lies? He has struggled to establish dominion over the Burning Hells and has turned to Sanctuary for a new source of power.

If so, I stand in awe of his strategy. I must learn from his actions. With only a fraction of his persuasive skills we could have endless numbers of mortals enacting our will without ever suspecting it. But one could never truly serve Belial, only be used by him. We would be pawns in his game, not partners in his glories.

He has infected the nobility of Caldeum.
He is too well protected to mark alone.

Despite all my efforts, I have not marked Azmodan's soul yet. I believe he has become aware of my master's plan—not because of any mistake, but because he can see the pieces being arranged on the board. He can read the plan from the movements of the pawns.

I doubt he will step foot on Sanctuary while the Black Soulstone exists. I will need help to subdue him in his domain.

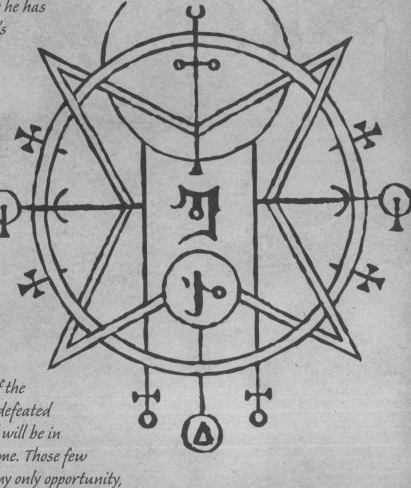

I have prepared the ritual. Though it lacks finesse and elegance, it will serve its purpose. But speed will be of the essence. When Azmodan is defeated in the Realm of Sin, his soul will be in a state of shock for a brief time. Those few vulnerable minutes will be my only opportunity, else his soul may enter the process of rebirth too quickly and be lost to me.

I have covertly drawn power from the Black Soulstone itself for this task. The ritual will be complex in its structure but fierce in its effect. I only need to bind the Soul of Sin into a cage with no rounded sides. Then he will be helpless.

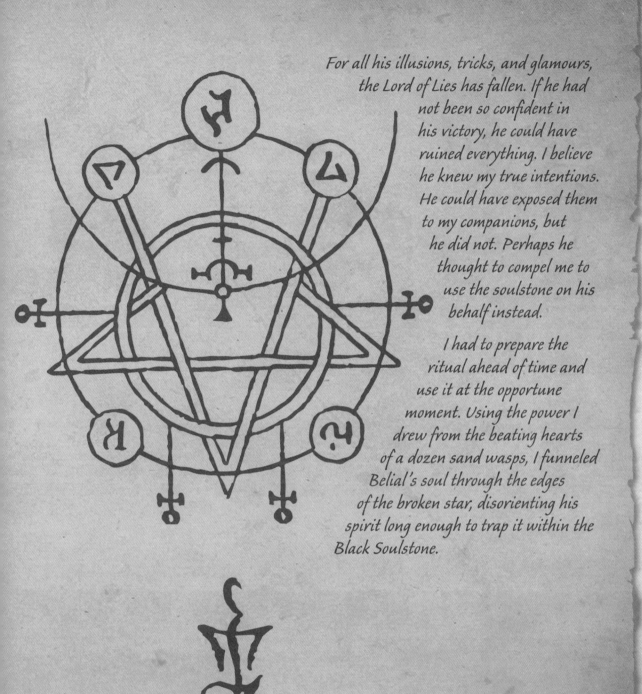

For all his illusions, tricks, and glamours, the Lord of Lies has fallen. If he had not been so confident in his victory, he could have ruined everything. I believe he knew my true intentions. He could have exposed them to my companions, but he did not. Perhaps he thought to compel me to use the soulstone on his behalf instead.

I had to prepare the ritual ahead of time and use it at the opportune moment. Using the power I drew from the beating hearts of a dozen sand wasps, I funneled Belial's soul through the edges of the broken star, disorienting his spirit long enough to trap it within the Black Soulstone.

Baal, Lord of Destruction

One of my first tasks in the Coven was to search for the resting place of Baal, known by his true name of Tor'Baalos. Once I learned that he was contained in the body of the Horadrim's old leader, Tal Rasha, it was only a matter of time before I found his tomb deep beneath the Aranoch deserts. It lay amid an array of false caverns and traps meant to ensnare any trespassers. Unfortunately, I could not learn how to enter the final chambers and free him. This angered me for quite some time.

The whispers in my dreams explained that I had done well in failure. Baal was a reckless force of annihilation, and after such a long period of imprisonment he was likely to kill any mortal who stood before him.

I believe that is the truth. Though I have no proof, I believe I have discerned another truth about the Lord of Destruction: it is by his will that the Eternal Conflict shall always rage. Even when he was exiled from the Burning Hells, he sought to corrupt all of Sanctuary. He did not do so because of any insight into humanity's potential, but because it existed and could be made into a weapon against the High Heavens.

What, then, would happen if the Lord of Destruction were victorious? What if he ground the High Heavens into ash? What if he destroyed Sanctuary and every other realm in existence? What would come after he lay the Burning Hells to ruin?

Would he destroy himself? Or would he be clever enough to never let it reach that point? Would he first embrace defeat, death, and rebirth, before risking an end to his cycle of annihilation?

These questions intrigue me. And they drive me ever forward.

Mephisto, Lord of Hatred

My first vision of the Burning Hells was the Realm of Hatred. It was as if I could feel the touch of Mephisto, or Dul'Mephistos, upon every mote of matter around me, even though the demon lord was not there.

I believe Mephisto is imprisoned in Travincal, beneath the sacred temples of the Zakarum. There is no other explanation for the seething hatred that courses through their ranks. Even imprisoned, the he has incredible power over humanity. Many of the Lords of Hell rely on force to enact their will; Mephisto can turn neighbor against neighbor for reasons that seem right and good. He can spur on conflict until there is only bloodshed that can be directed at his chosen targets.

Hatred even shapes the bonds between Mephisto and his closest followers. There are stories that his daughter, Lilith, rebelled against him and the Hells. She forged a pact with an angel known as Inarius. For what purpose, I do not know, but their forbidden union did not end well. Inarius was imprisoned in Mephisto's realm. Even now he languishes there, subjected to unending torture. Lilith has not been heard from since.

Was it hatred of her father that drove Lilith away? Or of all demons? Hatred is a powerful and simplifying force. The complexities of the world fall away when a heart is gripped by something as strong as hatred. It is a shame that mortals are blinded by its comforts.

Humans accept hatred as naturally as breathing. I am certainly not immune. As Zoltun Kulle claimed, we are all half-demon. If that is true, is there even a single force from the angels that we could wield as easily?

LILITH. Daughter of Hatred. Where is she? Whispers of a forbidden realm. The Abyss. Is she there?

Baal's soul is a restless, powerful entity. He caused so much chaos across Sanctuary after the destruction of the Worldstone that I thought he might succeed where my master failed.

Yet when he fell, his soul eagerly awaited my touch. He wishes to see the End of Days as much as his brother.

The power of destruction is not an easily controlled thing. My ritual did not attempt to do so. The central rune, carved into a human jawbone, amplified Baal's power, but the outer runes anchored it within the circle. I could feel a moment of pure satisfaction racing through his spirit, for the spell made him feel like he had just inhabited a new host body.

He quickly understood the truth, that I was imprisoning him until my master could make use of his spirit, but he did not lash out as I expected. I felt something close to amusement from him. I did not understand, but perhaps it is impossible to understand the ways of the Greater Evils.

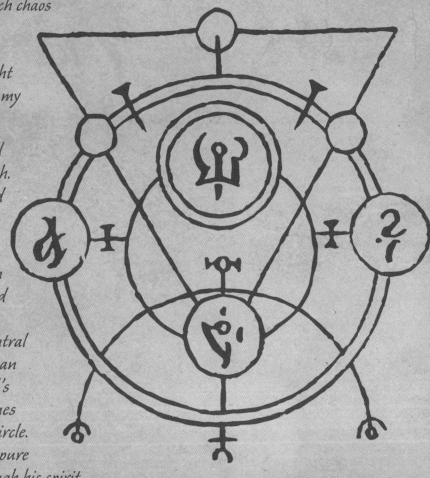

I marked Mephisto's soul after Baal. I think I had grown too confident. My master's plan had been working well, and I had accomplished things no any other human ever could.

When I found the Lord of Hatred's soul, it fought back with a rage that I had not anticipated. More than once, it seized control of my mind, and if my ritual did not have safeguards built into it, I would have been lost. Nevertheless, I completed my task.

Even in my arrogance, I still knew that hatred was a dangerous force. I left nothing to chance; I conducted the ritual with offerings from live human sacrifices, using fresh blood and organs to build the three-sided cage and the three anchors both inside and outside the circle. If I had used one less anchor or brought one less sacrifice, I would have failed.

Diablo, The Lord of Terror

Diablo, also called Al'Diabolos, has been depicted in many different physical forms. I myself have glimpsed him in dreams, though I do not know if what I saw was his true body or if it was a figment of my own inner fears.

Like his brothers, Mephisto and Baal, Diablo was imprisoned on our world. His spirit was locked in a crystal known as a soulstone. There are many rumors as to its current resting place. I do not know which one is true, but the thought of seeking it out fills me with dread.

My fear is natural. Wise, even. Every hidden history on Sanctuary—and beyond—regards Diablo as the most dangerous of all the Evils of the Burning Hells. His cunning surpasses any of the others, and he can corrupt or destroy at a whim . . . but it is his patience that makes him truly fearsome. Diablo has not once acted upon impulse or anger in all the histories of Sanctuary. He makes his plans, waits for the opportune moment, and strikes only when the time is right. And while he waits, he <u>ponders the possibility of failure and plans for it.</u>

When I first considered joining Diablo, I felt fear. He had not corrupted me, not yet, and I suspect he called me as his proof against failure.

Perhaps it was because he did not stoke my fears. He whispered of the End of Days, but only to pronounce me worthy to serve him in his ultimate victory. He gave me dreams of decay and corruption, but only because he knew I would see them as the natural end to humanity.

This was the simplest ritual, and the most difficult. The least dangerous, and the most important.

My master, Diablo, did not fight me when I marked his soul. His spirit caressed mine, but he did not resist. His plan is years away from completion, yet he is filled with confidence.

The ritual to mark his soul has nothing to do with containment. Soon, seven mighty souls will be drawn into the Black Soulstone, but only one will be in control. I created a dominant structure, one that bled outside the control of the circle, to ensure that the Lord of Terror's will would be unbound. It should be a simple matter for him to seize control of the soulstone's power.

The ritual, of course, was conducted with my own blood. Seemingly a river of it. The bloodline of the vessel comes from me. Now he has an affinity for it.

The final spell. I need more time to prepare, but have none. It is this or failure.

A purified iron blade should suffice to engrave the symbol on the Black Soulstone and keep the essences contained until the right time.

Duriel and Andariel, bound as one. Belial below them, always hidden in layers . . .

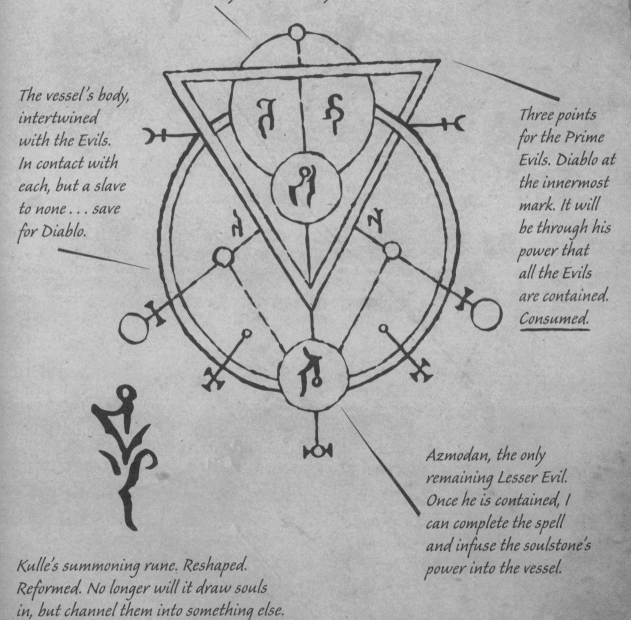

The vessel's body, intertwined with the Evils. In contact with each, but a slave to none . . . save for Diablo.

Three points for the Prime Evils. Diablo at the innermost mark. It will be through his power that all the Evils are contained. Consumed.

Azmodan, the only remaining Lesser Evil. Once he is contained, I can complete the spell and infuse the soulstone's power into the vessel.

Kulle's summoning rune. Reshaped. Reformed. No longer will it draw souls in, but channel them into something else.

The pieces are in place. The Black Soulstone
holds almost all the raging spirits of the Evils.

I sense the final gate approaching, and the key
is in my care. The vessel. She still sees me as
her mother, but that is not right. She was
born of me, but she is not mine. She is his.

She will become him.

Diablo, reborn.

The Seven made One.

The Prime Evil.

The Lord of the Burning Hells, the broken ruins
of Sanctuary, and the High Heavens.

And it will be my hand
that turns the key.

BLIZZARD ENTERTAINMENT

Written By: Robert Brooks and Matt Burns

Editors: Allison Irons, Diandra Lasrado, Paul Morrissey, David Wohl

Art Direction and Design: Bridget O'Neill

Creative Consultation: Luis Barriga, Matthew Berger, Victor Lee, Richie Marella, John Mueller, Fernando Pinilla, Jason Roberts

Lore Consultation: Sean Copeland, Christi Kugler, Justin Parker

Production: Brianne M. Loftis, Timothy Loughran, Alix Nicholaeff, Charlotte Racioppo, Derek Rosenberg, Cara Samuelsen, Jeffrey Wong

Director, Consumer Products: Byron Parnell

Director, Creative Development: Ralph Sanchez

CAMERON + COMPANY

Publisher: Chris Gruener

Creative Direction and Design: Iain R. Morris

Design Assistance: Noah Kay

Published by Blizzard Entertainment, Inc., Irvine, California, in 2018. No part of this book may be reproduced in any form without permission from the publisher.

Library of Congress Cataloging-in-Publication Data available.

ISBN: 978-1-945683-20-6

Manufactured in China

10 9 8 7 6 5 4 3 2 1

Cover by Christian Lichtner

Zoltan Boros: 10, 14, 19, 31, 81, 85, 92, 93, 96, 97, 107, 110, 111, 112, 113, 115, 130

Mark Gibbons: 6, 8, 22, 42, 43, 62, 73, 76, 142

Riccardo Federici: 141

Alex Horley: 74, 75

Bernie Kang: 20

Roman Kenney: 17, 27, 30, 34, 63, 70, 80, 84, 86, 106, 116

Joseph Lacroix: 18, 40, 72, 82, 114

Jean-Baptiste Monge: 32, 33, 36, 38, 39, 44, 45, 47, 48, 49, 54, 55, 60, 61, 64, 65, 66, 67, 68, 69, 79, 100, 101, 102, 103, 137

Fernando Pinilla: 13, 122, 123, 128, 129, 131, 134, 135, 136, 138, 139

Steve Prescott: 50, 51, 52, 53, 56, 57, 58, 59

Glenn Rane & John Polidora: 4, 5

Adrian Smith: 133

Josh Tallman: 15, 46, 71, 77, 78, 90, 91, 119, 120, 124, 125, 126, 127, 132

Konstantin Vavilov: 24, 25, 26, 28, 29, 35, 86, 87, 88, 89, 94, 95, 98, 99, 104, 105, 108, 109, 117

Page borders by Joseph Lacroix and Roman Kenney

Additional art by Joseph Lacroix, Roman Kenney and Fernando Pinilla